Teaching Literary Elements With

Short Stories

By Tara McCarthy

SCHOLASTIC
PROFESSIONAL BOOKS

New York • Toronto • London • Auckland • Sydney
Mexico City • New Delhi • Hong Kong

Acknowledgments

"La Bamba" by Gary Soto, from *Baseball in April and Other Stories* by Gary Soto. Copyright © 1990 by Gary Soto. Reprinted by permission of Harcourt Brace & Company.

"A Secret for Two" by Quentin Reynolds. Copyright © 1936. Used by permission of Beatrice Reynolds as Administratrix of the Reynolds Estate.

"How Many Stars in My Crown?" by Rosemary Wells, from *Mary on Horseback* by Rosemary Wells. Copyright © 1998 by Rosemary Wells. Used by permission of Dial Books for Young Readers, a division of Penguin Putnam, Inc.

"The Circuit" by Francisco Jimenez. Copyright © 1975. Used by permission of the author.

Cover design by Phyllis Rosenblatt
Cover illustrations by Laura H. Beith
Interior design by Sydney Wright

Table of Contents

Overview

Rationale ■

For many students, the sign that they've arrived in the land of the "grown-up reader" is their ability to read novels and chapter books on their own. Why, then, should you engage your students in reading short stories?

One reason is the pleasure of enjoying a story as a group. Another reason—and the focus of this book—is that exploring a short story with your students allows you to teach literary elements in a controlled and concise manner.

Short stories incorporate many basic literary elements

Main character, setting, conflict, plot, symbols, and theme—these are all examples of story elements. These elements, of course, appear in novels and chapter books. They also appear in short stories. However, in a short story, determining these elements takes less time, for the reading experience is shorter.

All students participate in learning

Exploring short stories as a class activity insures that every student participates in the discovery process. Most short stories can be shared in one or two classroom periods. This makes the reading more controllable, for you do not need to rely on students completing a story as a homework assignment.

Input and feedback are immediate

Through immediate follow-up in the classroom, you and your students can focus as a group on the literary elements you wish to stress.

In addition, you and your students can benefit from short stories in these areas:

◆ You can informally assess reading and comprehension skills. Students' oral reading and discussion give you an opportunity to identify areas where individual students may need follow-up instruction.

- Students might already have experience with studying short stories, for the short-story genre can include fairy tales, folktales, and even picture books they've enjoyed over the years.
- The short-story form gives students a realistic writing model. When we ask students to "write a story," we usually mean a short story, not a novel. By sharing and analyzing literary elements as they appear in short stories, students will find examples they can follow as they plan and write their own.

Book Highlights ▪

This book contains four complete short stories along with suggested strategies to discuss and explore each. You will also find ways to expand the readings into writing exercises.

The Short Stories

Each story in this book can be presented to your class in its entirety. Reproduce the stories so each student has a copy. You might choose to browse the stories first. Present them in the sequence given, if you wish, but feel free to choose the stories that best suit your needs. For example, if you are studying regional U.S. history, you may choose to present "How Many Stars in My Crown?"

Margin Notes

In the margin of each story, you will find call-out notes. These notes signal places where you and your students can pause briefly in the shared oral reading to check comprehension and focus on specific literary elements.

Before Reading

For each story, a pre-reading activity is suggested to build students' interest and to help them draw on their own experiences and prior knowledge. These pre-reading activities involve graphic organizers. Re-create the organizers on the chalkboard or on chart paper, challenging students to help you complete them.

After Reading

After-reading activities encourage students to:
- respond personally to the story;
- focus on specific literary elements of the story;
- retell and expand on the story;
- plan, write, and share their own stories.

Reader/Writer Notebook Pages

After the last short-story chapter, you will find a section of reproducible activity sheets. These sheets provide a way for students to organize their copies of the four stories in this book, as well as to organize, refer to, and share what they discover as they read and write. Ideally, each student should have a three-ring binder in which to store the Reader/Writer Notebook sheets. If possible, you might reproduce each introductory activity sheet in a different color to make referencing easier. Colored label tabs work well too.

As students explore each story, make sure they fill out the appropriate areas on the introductory activity sheets. This will help them gather their thoughts and evaluate literary elements. Then have them file their completed activity sheets related to each story in the appropriate sections of their Reader/Writer Notebooks. Make sure students have access to a three-hole punch.

General Procedures ▪

It is not necessary to follow the exact sequence of activities for each short story. However, activities do build slightly upon each other. If you feel your students are proficient in one area, feel free to skip ahead. Or incorporate an idea you applied successfully to one short story that your students enjoyed in teaching another. Gauge students' responsiveness and interest to guide how you use the activities. Here are some suggestions.

Before You Implement This Book

◆ Help students get together their Reader/Writer Notebooks. Make sure each student has a three-ring binder. Then reproduce and pass out copies of the Reader/Writer Notebook pages. Show students how to organize them in their binders.

◆ If possible, you might also share with students the glossary in this book. Reproduce and pass out pages 90–92. Let students place the glossary pages in their binders. This will allow them to immediately look up any literary elements they find confusing.

◆ Talk with students about reading short stories and understanding literary elements.

Before You Undertake Each Story

◆ Reproduce the short story and the corresponding activity sheets. Make sure you have enough copies so each student in your class has one.

◆ Skim the Present the Story, Read the Story, and Analyze the Story activities. Prepare any visuals you may wish to use, such as graphic organizers that guide class discussions.

Applying Literary Elements

◆ Each chapter ends with activities to help students write their own short stories. The activities focus on literary elements explored in each short story they explored.

◆ Incorporating literary elements into their writing is an excellent way to assess students' understanding of literary elements. Filling in the story planning sheets will help with assessment.

Time Management ▪

The time you take to cover each story and its follow-ups will, of course, depend on the overall reading and writing abilities of your students. Here is a five-day sequence to guide your approach.

Day 1.
Involve the class in the prereading activities.
Read the story together.
Invite students to share their Personal Responses.

Day 2.
Explore the Literal Response activities.
Continue with the Challenge activity.

Day 3.
Engage the class in the Retell the Story and/or the Expand the Story activities.

Day 4.
Invite students to Plan an Original Story. Provide for ample writing time.

Day 5.
Encourage students in the Share Your Writing activities.

Reading the Stories ▪

Short stories can be shared and explored in a group setting in many ways. Decide which oral-reading technique you'd like to apply. Your shared reading could also involve more than one technique. Here are some examples.

Oral-Reading Techniques

Share-Pairs

Begin the reading by reading aloud the first paragraph or section. Then ask an accomplished student reader to read the next paragraph. Continue by reading the following paragraph yourself, then asking a second student to read the next.

Repeat-Reads

After you or an accomplished student reader reads a section, invite another student to read the same section. In the second reading, ask the student to stress the words or phrases she or he considers especially important. In this way, second readers not only get valuable oral-reading practice but they share their insights with classmates.

Summary-Staters

After you or a student reads two or three paragraphs aloud, encourage another student to summarize, in one or two sentences, the main idea of those paragraphs. This strategy allows you to check not only general comprehension but the students' grasp of literary elements.

Teacher-Reads

Read the entire story aloud to the class, encouraging students to follow along silently with their copies. This technique allows students to hear the pronunciation of difficult or unfamiliar words. It also prepares them for reading the story again on their own. After you read the story, presenting students with an oral model, they might feel more comfortable reading aloud in class.

Teachers as Readers

As you work with the class, don't be reluctant to model what a good reader does. Involve yourself in the discussions, not so much as a teacher but as a student. Explain that you are exploring the story along with them. You are trying to determine the literary elements just as they are. Your students will benefit greatly by seeing that a good story engages the attention of adults as well as students. Here are a few pointers:

◆ When necessary, keep the class discussion moving by sharing your own insights about the character, the plot, the setting, and other literary elements.

◆ Conclude a discussion by sharing what you've learned as you listened to students' own ideas and responses.

◆ If possible, ahead of time, complete for yourself the reproducible that students will be asked to complete that day. This will enable you to preview and appreciate the task students are asked to do.

◆ Provide other examples of short stories for students to read and analyze on their own or with partners. The bibliography on pages 93–96 suggests books you might include in your classroom. Encourage students to add to the collection with short stories they write themselves. For extra incentive, you might include any stories that you, yourself, have written.

Summing Up ▪

This book aims to provide your students not only with examples of great short stories but also with the common vocabulary to discuss them (*plot, character, resolution,* and so on). Chapter titles refer to those elements that are prominent in each story. However, most elements can be investigated in each story too. Keep in mind that identifying, analyzing, and applying the elements of literature is hard work. That's why the activities for each story may return to and review elements previously explored.

Devoted readers and writers discover—even over a lifetime of working with literature—that recognizing and applying literary elements is an ongoing challenge. Don't expect your students—or yourself—to "master" the elements by reading only one short story. The goal here is not complete mastery but the thrill of the quest!

In this regard, consider what the writer Thomas Mann had to say:

> Writers are people for whom writing is more
> difficult than it is for other people.

Relate this to short stories. The difficulty lies in that a good story—short or long—must include all the elements of literature. When readers, such as your students, know what these elements are and can identify and discuss them in a short story, they will appreciate the story more. And, as a bonus, students are inspired to undertake the happy difficulty of incorporating key literary elements as they write short stories of their own.

Character

One of the most important features of a story is the main character. The main character is the focus and, therefore, the force that moves the story along. Without an understanding of the main character's personality and growth, a story can be meaningless to the reader. To help students explore character development and the literary elements involved, invite them to read "La Bamba" by Gary Soto.

Story Summary ▪▪▪

Fifth grader Manuel Gomez volunteers for a school talent show. He will lip-synch and dance to a recording of the song "La Bamba." Manuel hopes to impress his family and a girl he likes, but he also has doubts about his performance. While in the middle of his routine, the "La Bamba" record gets stuck, playing the same phrase over and over. Manuel, confused but determined, repeats the dance steps and continues to mouth the lyrics, until the faulty record is removed. Feeling humiliated, he's surprised by the audience's wild applause. It turns out that Manuel's quick-thinking cover-up was so skillful that the audience believed the repetition was intentional.

Literary Elements—Character Development ▪▪▪

As students enjoy Manuel's story, they will explore these literary elements and focus on the character development of Manuel.

◆ **Motivation.** What motivates Manuel to want to be in the talent show? What does this tell the reader about the type of person Manuel is?

◆ **Conflict.** What conflicting feelings does Manuel have about the talent show? What does this tell the reader about the type of person Manuel is?

◆ **Problem/Solution.** What problem does Manuel face when performing? How does he solve the problem? What does this tell us about Manuel?

◆ **Resolution.** How does Manuel feel after the performance? How has Manuel grown as a character? How has Manuel changed since readers first met him?

La Bamba

by Gary Soto

Manuel was the fourth of seven children and looked like a lot of kids in his neighborhood: black hair, brown face, and skinny legs scuffed from summer play. But summer was giving way to fall: the trees were turning red, the lawns brown, and the pomegranate trees were heavy with fruit. Manuel walked to school in the frosty morning, kicking leaves and thinking of tomorrow's talent show. He was still amazed that he had volunteered. He was going to pretend to sing Richie Valens's "La Bamba" before the entire school.

1. Who is the <u>main character</u>?

Why did I raise my hand? he asked himself, but in his heart he knew the answer. He yearned for the limelight. He wanted applause as loud as a thunderstorm, and to hear his friends say, "Man, that was bad!" And he wanted to impress the girls, especially Petra Lopez, the second-prettiest girl in his class. The first was already taken by his friend Ernie. Manuel knew he should be reasonable, since he himself was not great-looking, just average.

2. What is Manuel's <u>motivation</u>, or reason, for signing up for the talent show?

Manuel kicked through the fresh-fallen leaves. When he got to school he realized he had forgotten his math workbook. If his teacher found out, he would have to stay after school and miss practice for the talent show. But fortunately for him, they did drills that morning.

During lunch Manuel hung around with Benny, who was also in the talent show. Benny was going to play the trumpet in spite of the fat lip he had gotten playing football.

"How do I look?" Manuel asked. He cleared his throat and started moving his lips in pantomime. No words came out, just a hiss that sounded like a snake. Manuel tried to look emotional, flailing his arms on the high notes and opening his eyes and mouth as wide as he could when he came to "*Para bailar la baaaaammmba.*" *

After Manuel finished, Benny said it looked all right, but suggested Manuel dance while he sang. Manuel thought for a moment and decided it was a good idea.

"Yeah, just think you're like Michael Jackson or someone like that," Benny suggested. "But don't get carried away."

During rehearsal, Mr. Roybal, nervous about his debut as the school's talent coordinator, cursed under his breath when the lever that controlled the speed of the record player jammed.

"Darn," he growled, trying to force the lever. "What's wrong with you?"

"Is it broken?" Manuel asked, bending over for a closer look. It looked all right to him.

Mr. Roybal assured Manuel that he would have a good record player at the talent show, even if it meant bringing his own stereo from home.

Manuel sat in a folding chair, twirling his record on his thumb. He watched a skit about personal hygiene, a mother-and-daughter violin duo, five first-grade girls jumping rope, a karate kid breaking boards, three girls singing "Like a Virgin," and a skit about the pilgrims. If the record player hadn't been broken, he would have gone after the karate kid, an easy act to follow, he told himself.

As he twirled his forty-five record, Manuel thought they had a great talent show. The entire school would be amazed. His mother and father would be proud, and his brothers and sisters would be jealous and pout. It would be a night to remember.

Benny walked on stage, raised his trumpet to his mouth, and waited for his cue. Mr. Roybal raised his hand like a symphony conductor and let it fall dramatically. Benny inhaled and blew so loud that Manuel dropped his record, which rolled across the cafeteria floor until it hit a wall. Manuel raced after it, picked it up, and wiped it clean.

"Boy, I'm glad it didn't break," he said with a sigh.

** *Para bailar la bamba:* (in order) to dance the la bamba

13

3. Manuel has a <u>conflict</u>: He's shy about performing but also <u>wants</u> to perform.

That night Manuel had to do the dishes and a lot of homework, so he could only practice in the shower. In bed he prayed that he wouldn't mess up. He prayed that it wouldn't be like when he was a first-grader. For Science Week he had wired together a C battery and a bulb, and told everyone he had discovered how a flashlight worked. He was so pleased with himself that he practiced for hours pressing the wire to the battery, making the bulb wink a dim, orange-ish light. He showed it to so many kids in his neighborhood that when it was time to show his class how a flashlight worked, the battery was dead. He pressed the wire to the battery, but the bulb didn't respond. He pressed until his thumb hurt and some kids in the back started snickering.

But Manuel fell asleep confident that nothing would go wrong this time.

The next morning his father and mother beamed at him. They were proud that he was going to be in the talent show.

"I wish you would tell us what you're doing," his mother said. His father, a pharmacist who wore a blue smock with his name in a plastic rectangle, looked up from the newspaper and sided with his wife. "Yes, what are you doing in the talent show?"

"You'll see," said Manuel with his mouth full of Cheerios.

The day whizzed by, and so did his afternoon chores and dinner. Suddenly he was dressed in his best clothes and standing next to Benny backstage, listening to the commotion as the cafeteria filled with school kids and parents. The lights dimmed, and Mr. Roybal, sweaty in a tight suit and a necktie with a large knot, wet his lips and parted the stage curtains.

"Good evening, everyone," the kids behind the curtain heard him say. "Good evening to you," some of the smart-alecky kids said back to him.

"Tonight we bring you the best John Burroughs Elementary has to offer, and I'm sure that you'll be both pleased and amazed that our little school houses so much talent. And now, without further ado, let's get on with the show." He turned and, with a swish of his hand, commanded, "Part the curtain." The curtain parted in jerks. A girl dressed as a toothbrush and a boy dressed as a dirty gray tooth walked onto the stage and sang:

> *Brush, brush, brush*
> *Floss, floss, floss*
> *Gargle the germs away—hey! hey! hey!*

After they finished singing, they turned to Mr. Roybal, who dropped his hand. The toothbrush dashed around the stage after the dirty tooth, which was laughing and having a great time until it slipped and nearly rolled off the stage.

Mr. Roybal jumped out and caught it just in time. "Are you OK?"

The dirty tooth answered, "Ask my dentist," which drew laughter and applause from the audience.

The violin duo played next, and except for one time when the girl got lost, they sounded fine. People applauded, and some even stood up. Then the first-grade girls maneuvered onto the stage while jumping rope. They were all smiles and bouncing ponytails as a hundred cameras flashed at once. Mothers "aahed" and fathers sat up proudly.

The karate kid was next. He did a few kicks, yells, and chops, and finally, when his father held up a board, punched it in two. The audience clapped and looked at each other, wide-eyed with respect. The boy bowed to the audience, and father and son ran off the stage.

Manuel remained behind the stage shivering with fear. He mouthed the words to "La Bamba" and swayed from left to right. Why did he raise his hand and volunteer? Why couldn't he have just sat there like the rest of the kids and not said anything? While the karate kid was on stage, Mr. Roybal, more sweaty than before, took Manuel's forty-five record and placed it on the new record player.

"You ready?" Mr. Roybal asked.

"Yeah . . ."

Mr. Roybal walked back on stage and announced that Manuel Gomez, a fifth-grader in Mrs. Knight's class, was going to pantomime Richie Valens's classic hit "La Bamba."

The cafeteria roared with applause. Manuel was nervous but loved the noisy crowd. He pictured his mother and father applauding loudly and his brothers and sisters also clapping, though not as energetically.

Manuel walked on stage and the song started immediately. Glassy-eyed from the shock of being in front of so many people, Manuel moved his lips and swayed in a made-up dance step. He couldn't see his parents, but he could see his brother Mario, who was a year younger, thumb-wrestling with a friend. Mario was wearing Manuel's favorite shirt; he would deal with Mario later. He saw some other kids get up and head for the drinking fountain, and a baby sitting in the middle of an aisle sucking her thumb and watching him intently.

What am I doing here? thought Manuel. This is no fun at all. Everyone was just sitting there. Some people were moving to the beat, but most were just watching him, like they would a monkey at the zoo.

But when Manuel did a fancy dance step, there was a burst of applause and some girls screamed. Manuel tried another dance step. He heard more applause and screams and started getting into the groove as he shivered and snaked like Michael Jackson around the stage. But the record got stuck, and he had to sing

Para bailar la bamba
Para bailar la bamba
Para bailar la bamba
Para bailar la bamba

again and again.

Manuel couldn't believe his bad luck. The audience began to laugh and stand up in their chairs. Manuel remembered how the forty-five record had dropped from his hand and rolled across the cafeteria floor. It probably got scratched, he thought, and now it was stuck, and he was stuck dancing and moving his lips to the same words over and over. He had never been so embarrassed. He would have to ask his parents to move the family out of town.

After Mr. Roybal ripped the needle across the record, Manuel slowed his dance steps to a halt. He didn't know what to do except bow to the audience, which applauded wildly, and scoot off the stage, on the verge of tears. This was worse than the homemade flashlight. At least no one laughed then, they just snickered.

Manuel stood alone, trying hard to hold back the tears as Benny, center stage, played his trumpet. Manuel was jealous because he

4. Complication! The record sticks! What are Manuel's choices at this point?

5. Climax! What big decision does Manuel make?

sounded great, then mad as he recalled that it was Benny's loud trumpet playing that made the forty-five record fly out of his hands. But when the entire cast lined up for a curtain call, Manuel received a burst of applause that was so loud it shook the walls of the cafeteria. Later, as he mingled with the kids and parents, everyone patted him on the shoulder and told him, "Way to go. You were really funny."

Funny? Manuel thought. Did he do something funny?

6. The resolution is how a story turns out as a result of the big decision. How do things turn out for Manuel?

Funny. Crazy. Hilarious. These were the words people said to him. He was confused, but beyond caring. All he knew was that people were paying attention to him, and his brothers and sisters looked at him with a mixture of jealousy and awe. He was going to pull Mario aside and punch him in the arm for wearing his shirt, but he cooled it. He was enjoying the limelight. A teacher brought him cookies and punch, and the popular kids who had never before given him the time of day now clustered around him. Ricardo, the editor of the school bulletin, asked him how he made the needle stick.

"It just happened," Manuel said, crunching on a star-shaped cookie.

At home that night his father, eager to undo the buttons on his shirt and ease into his La-Z-Boy recliner, asked Manuel the same thing, how he managed to make the song stick on the words "*Para bailar la bamba.*"

Manuel thought quickly and reached for scientific jargon he had read in magazines. "Easy, Dad. I used laser tracking with high optics and low functional decibels per channel." His proud but confused father told him to be quiet and go to bed.

"*Ah, que niños tan truchas,*" * he said as he walked to the kitchen for a glass of milk. "I don't know how you kids nowadays get so smart."

Manuel, feeling happy, went to his bedroom, undressed, and slipped into his pajamas. He looked in the mirror and began to pantomime "La Bamba," but stopped because he was tired of the song. He crawled into bed. The sheets were as cold as the moon that stood over the peach tree in their backyard.

He was relieved that the day was over. Next year, when they asked for volunteers for the talent show, he wouldn't raise his hand. Probably.

* *Que niños tan truchas:* Children are clever.

Present the Story

Contrast Chart ■ ■ ■

Prepare students for reading by explaining that "La Bamba" is the story of a student who agrees to participate in a school talent show. Talk with students about what a talent show entails. Why might a talent show be fun for the audience? For the participants? How else might the participants feel? Brainstorm with students a list of pleasant and unpleasant experiences that the main character in "La Bamba" might face. Record their ideas on a chart, like the one below, for students to refer to later as they plan their own stories.

WHAT MIGHT HAPPEN AT A TALENT SHOW	
Good Things	**Unpleasant Things**
You don't make any mistakes.	You could forget your lines.
You might win a prize.	People could laugh at you.
Your friends might praise you.	Nobody claps.

Distribute Copies of the Story ■ ■ ■

Let students briefly flip through the story. Draw their attention to the notes in the margin. Explain that these notes indicate places where you will ask them to pause in their reading to review and discuss story elements. Point out that some words in the margin notes are underlined. Mention that these underlined words are the literary elements specific to that margin note.

Read the Story

As students read the story together, refer to the margin notes to guide discussion.

Margin Note 1:
Who is the <u>Main Character</u>?

Student Response: Manuel.

Further Discussion: As the story progresses, elicit from students the names of other characters that are important to the story. For example:

◆ Benny: Playing his trumpet, Benny causes Manuel to drop his "La Bamba" record and scratch it. In turn, this causes the record to stick during Manuel's performance.

◆ Mr. Roybal: The talent-show coordinator.

◆ Manuel's family: Manuel wishes to make his parents proud while at the same time make his siblings envious of his performance.

◆ The talent-show audience: Manuel judges his performance based on their reaction.

Margin Note 2:
What is Manuel's <u>motivation</u>, or reason, for signing up for the talent show?

Student Response: He wants to impress his family and a girl he likes.

Margin Note 3:
Manuel has a <u>conflict</u>: He's shy about performing, but also wants to perform.

Further Discussion: Ask students to consider if this conflict seems realistic. In other words, have there been times in their lives when they've wished to show others what they can do, yet have also been a little reluctant to do so? Why did they feel this way? Why might Manuel feel this way? What does this say about Manuel's character?

Margin Note 4:
<u>Complication</u>! The record sticks! What are Manuel's choices at this point?

Student Response: Students may suggest: Leave the stage. Stop and yell at Mr. Roybal. Somehow continue with his performance.

Margin Note 5:
<u>Climax</u>! What big decision does Manuel make?

Student Response: He decides to stay on the stage and continue his performance.

Margin Note 6:

The <u>resolution</u> is how a story turns out as a result of the decision. How do things turn out for Manuel?

Student Response: Even though his talent-show performance didn't go as planned, Manuel feels good about himself, for the audience enjoyed the show and his parents are proud.

Analyze the Story— As a Group

Affective Response ■ ■ ■

Reproduce and pass out copies of Personal Responses on page 26. Go over each question with the class. Encourage students to discuss the questions as a group. Then ask students to complete the activity sheet on their own.

On the chalkboard, draw a "report card" for Manuel, like the one shown here. Help students explore Manuel as a character as they consider what grade Manuel should receive for his actions in the story. (For example, E= Excellent; S= Satisfactory; I= Needs Improvement.) In the Comments column of the chart, challenge students to provide reasons for the grades they give Manuel.

Name: Manuel Gomez		
Personal Quality	**Grade**	**Comments**
Persistence		
Responsibility		
Confidence		
Friendship		

Literal Response ■ ■ ■

Reproduce and pass out the graphic organizer Organizing Literary Elements on page 27. Preview the prompts, or headings. Let the class work together so students can exchange ideas about the literary elements that build Manuel as a character. Or challenge partners to tackle the page, then encourage them to compare and amend their responses with those of other groups.

Challenge: Write a One-Sentence Story Summary ■ ■ ■

To summarize a story in one sentence is, indeed, a challenge. Present students with that challenge. Explain that their sentences must clearly identify the main character, the conflict, and the climax. The value of the challenge is that:

◆ The teacher gets a quick, informal view of students' comprehension of the story as a whole, making assessment easier.

◆ Students must focus on three essential literary elements.

◆ Students get practice planning how to build those literary elements into stories they write.

You may want to incorporate the one-sentence-summary approach each time students read a short story. Below is the general procedure, using "La Bamba" as a model.

One-Sentence Story Summary ■ ■ ■

1. On the chalkboard, list the three literary elements you wish to focus on.
Character
Conflict
Resolution

2. Help students identify each.
Character: Manuel
Conflict: Wanting to perform well in the talent show; nervous about the talent show.
Resolution: He is a success, even though things do not go as planned.

3. Model how to incorporate each element into one sentence.

Manuel (character) is excited, yet nervous, about performing in the school talent show (conflict), but he successfully performs and feels good about himself, even with a few problems (resolution).

4. Review with students what the one-sentence summary does:
◆ identifies the main character;
◆ presents the conflict the character faces;
◆ describes the resolution of the character's conflict;
◆ does not begin with "This story is about...."

5. If possible, help students compose a one-sentence summary for another story they have read. Let them choose the story. Following is one more example to guide the activity. It is based on the book "My Brother Sam Is Dead" by James Lincoln Collier and Christopher Collier.

> *During the American Revolution, a boy* (character) *can't decide which soldiers to support* (conflict) *and ultimately learns that in a war nobody really wins* (resolution).

6. As a follow-up and to assess students' understanding of a one-sentence summary, challenge students, either independently or in small groups, to write one-sentence summaries for other stories the class has enjoyed. Invite the groups to read their summaries aloud, then challenge the rest of the class to identify the stories on which they are based. Point out that those summaries that are concise enable classmates to guess the story right away.

Analyze the Story— On Their Own

Retell the Story—Plot Points ■ ■ ■

To focus on plot, invite students to:

◆ Write entries for a daily journal Manuel might keep as he prepares for and performs in the talent show. With a partner, invite the student to present the entries in a readers theater format.

◆ Draw and display a comic-strip panel, complete with dialogue balloons, that shows and tells in sequence what Manuel experiences as he performs onstage.

Retell the Story—Another Format ■ ■ ■

By retelling the story in a different format, students will hone not only writing skills but creative-thinking skills as well. For example, students could retell Manuel's story as a newspaper article, as dialogue between a reporter and Manuel, as a nonfiction piece that explores how to overcome conflicts. Or Manuel's story could also be told as poetry, as shown below. If time allows, let students explore another form of writing, one that piques their interest.

Poem based on "La Bamba"
Manuel takes a real big chance.
He volunteers to sing and dance.
The record sticks! What will he do?
Leave the stage or see it through?
This boy is brave, and that's a fact!
He goes right on with his dancing act.
He leaves the stage. He's close to tears.
But the audience cheers and cheers!
They think his act was planned that way.
This was Manuel's big day!

Expand the Story ▪ ▪ ▪

To focus on character development, encourage students to:

◆ Write a "next-time" tale about Manuel. Prompt their ideas with thought-provoking questions, such as: From what you now know about Manuel, what do you think he will do next year when it's time for the annual talent show? Will he perform? If not, what will he say to his family, friends, and Mr. Roybal? If yes, what will he do in the talent show? Write a new story for Manuel, or share your story idea aloud with classmates.

Plan an Original Story ▪ ▪ ▪

Help students recognize that what makes the short story "La Bamba" enjoyable is the well-developed main character of Manuel. Point out that Manuel and his situation is interesting because Manuel faces a conflict. To review the conflict, inform students that they actually discussed it *before* reading the story. Display the What Might Happen at a Talent Show chart they generated before reading. Explain that the "good things" and the "unpleasant things" were all part of the conflict that Manuel had within himself when he thought about the talent show. Conclude that developing a character with a compelling conflict will help them write a better story.

Then reproduce and pass out the Developing a Main Character graphic organizer on page 28. Review with students the components of the chart. Then encourage each student to combine and play with ideas to develop a main character, a situation, and a conflict for an original story. As ideas come to them, suggest that they write a one-sentence summary of the proposed story that they can refer to as they write.

To provide further inspiration for strong story characters for compelling stories, you might have students look to real life for ideas. Let students search newspapers or magazines for intriguing headlines. Or, ahead of time, collect a few headlines for students to examine. Discuss with students the characters and stories the headlines might inspire. Below are some fictional headlines you might employ to help focus on a specific literary element.

Man Claims to Be 125 Years Old

Literary Element: Conflict

Think About It: Who is this man? What does he look like? Where does he live? What does he know about things that happened long ago? What proof does he have of his age? What jobs has he held? Why might he want to keep his life private? Why might he want to tell others about his life?

Write About It: Write a paragraph that describes the 125-year-old man, focusing on his internal conflict about talking about his life. Incorporate your ideas from "Think About It."

Garbage Dump Is Site of Dinosaur Fossils

Literary Element: Motivation

Think About It: Who claims to have found the fossils? Where is the garbage dump? What does it look like? sound like? smell like? Are the fossils real or fake? Why might someone announce to the world that they have found such fossils?

Write About It: Write a paragraph about the person who found the fossils, explaining how the fossils were found and what motivated the person to share the findings with the world. Incorporate your ideas from "Think About It."

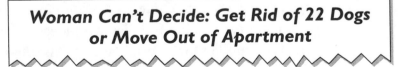

Woman Can't Decide: Get Rid of 22 Dogs or Move Out of Apartment

Literary Element: Problem/Solution

Think About It: How did the woman acquire 22 dogs? Why does she want to keep them? Why does she need to get rid of them? How is this a problem? Why does the woman want to stay in her present home? Where else could she go with her 22 dogs?

Write About It: Write a paragraph describing the woman's thoughts and actions as she deals with the problem and arrives at a solution. Incorporate your ideas from "Think About It."

Another exciting place for students to find strong character ideas about which to base a short story is a narrative, or storytelling, poem. Share a few with the class. These can be classic tales, like the Robin Hood ballads, or funny, modern verses, like those of Shel Silverstein or Jack Prelutsky. Discuss the main character or characters of the poem as well as the character's motives, conflicts, and/or problems. Suggest to students that they create a story character based on the character in the poem that faces similar conflicts or problems.

Share Your Writing ■ ■ ■

Let students review, assess, and revise their stories following the traditional Writing Partner procedure. (See the Writing Partner Conference reproducible on page 87). Or try the following:

Free Read. Invite the writer to read the story aloud to a small group. Instruct the listeners not to comment. Instead, they are merely to listen to the story, to the flow of ideas and language. The writer should also listen to the words, becoming his or her own audience. The value of a free read is that the writers learn about their work from reading it aloud. By hearing the story, rather than just reading it, the writer can note strong points and weak points of the work, including character development, plot, and language. This will help the writer formulate ideas for how to revise and improve the story.

Reader/Writer Notebook ■ ■ ■

Invite students to record the story in a reader or writer notebook. This way they can refer to the story again, review literary elements, and guide their own writing activities. Page 7 in the intro explains each step and reproducible involved in the Reader/Writer Notebook. Refer to those pages as a means of culminating your exploration of literary elements in "La Bamba." Repeat the procedure with the other short stories in this book.

Personal Responses

1. What part of "La Bamba" most grabbed your attention? Why did that part interest you?

_____

_____

_____

_____

_____

2. How did you feel when the record stuck during Manuel's performance?

_____

_____

_____

_____

_____

_____

_____

3. Do you think Manuel's performance is believable? Explain your answer.

_____

_____

_____

_____

_____

4. Describe an incident in which you or someone you know had to do some quick thinking to solve a problem.

_____

_____

_____

_____

_____

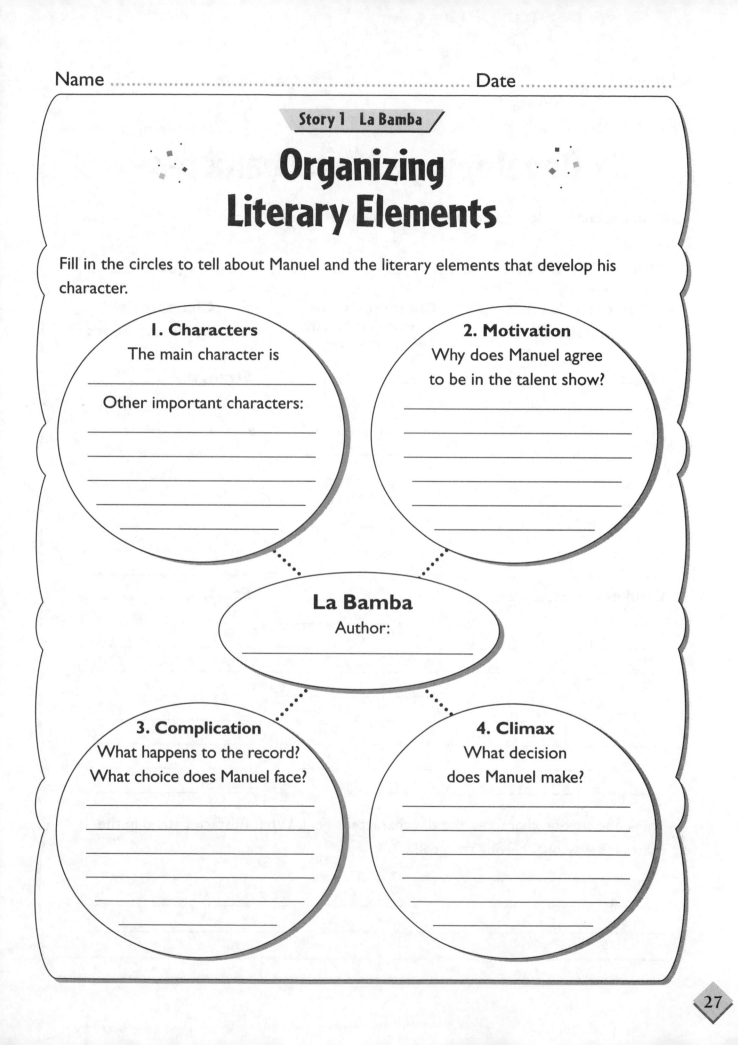

Story 1 La Bamba

Organizing Literary Elements

Fill in the circles to tell about Manuel and the literary elements that develop his character.

1. Characters

The main character is

_____

Other important characters:

_____

_____

_____

_____

_____

2. Motivation

Why does Manuel agree to be in the talent show?

_____

_____

_____

_____

_____

La Bamba

Author:

_____

3. Complication

What happens to the record? What choice does Manuel face?

_____

_____

_____

_____

_____

4. Climax

What decision does Manuel make?

_____

_____

_____

_____

Name .... Date ....

Developing a Main Character

Fill in the chart below to create a story character of your own.

Character's Name: _____ **Age:** _____

Character's Likes and Dislikes	Character's Goal (or what the character wants to achieve)	Character's Strengths and Fears
Likes: _____	_____	Strengths: _____
_____	_____	_____
_____	_____	_____
_____	_____	_____
_____	_____	_____
_____	_____	_____
_____	_____	_____
_____	_____	_____
Dislikes: _____	_____	Fears: _____
_____	_____	_____
_____	_____	_____
_____	_____	_____
_____	_____	_____
_____	_____	_____
_____	_____	_____

Think about your character and the character's goal. What obstacles stand in the charcter's way of achieving the goal?

_____

_____

_____

_____

Setting

The setting is the backdrop of a story. It can define the actions of the characters, as well as paint an inspiring canvas against which the characters relate, move, and deal with their conflicts and problems. The setting transports readers to places only in their imaginations, including exotic locales and periods of the past. To help students investigate story setting and the literary elements involved, invite them to read "A Secret for Two" by Quentin Reynolds.

Story Summary ▪ ▪ ▪

Pierre has worked for many years as a milkman in Montreal, making deliveries to his longtime customers. His milk wagon is drawn by a horse named Joseph, who has learned the route so well that he stops by instinct. Together, Pierre and Joseph demonstrate a love, trust, and efficiency that is compelling to all. One morning, Pierre learns that Joseph has died. Distraught by the news, Pierre stumbles into the street, where he is hit and killed by a truck. Only then do we learn that Pierre has been blind for years. Because Joseph knew the milk route so well, Pierre's blindness was a secret between the two.

Literary Elements—Setting ▪ ▪ ▪

As students appreciate Pierre's story, they will explore literary elements that build the story setting.

◆ **Location.** In which country does this story take place? How does this add to the story?

◆ **Time Period.** Does this story take place in the past or the present? Why could it not take place in the present? How does the time period add to the story?

◆ **Atmosphere.** How would you describe the atmosphere of the story? For example, is it friendly? kind? frightening? anxious?

◆ **Ethnic Details:** To make a setting come alive, stories often include words that reflect a culture, such as simple phrases in foreign languages and food names. Character names may also reflect ethnic background.

A Secret for Two

by Quentin Reynolds

1. The location and time period of a story is the <u>setting</u>. Where and when does this story take place? How do you know?

Montreal is a very large city, but, like all cities, it has some very small streets. Streets, for instance, like Prince Edward Street, which is only four blocks long, ending in a *cul-de-sac.** No one knew Prince Edward Street as well as did Pierre Dupin, for Pierre had delivered milk to the families on the street for thirty years now.

During the past fifteen years the horse which drew the milk wagon used by Pierre was a large white horse named Joseph. In Montreal, especially in that part of Montreal which is very French, the animals, like children, are often given the names of saints. When the big white horse first came to the Provincale Milk Company he didn't have a name. They told Pierre that he could use the white horse henceforth. Pierre stroked the softness of the horse's neck; he stroked the sheen of its splendid belly and he looked into the eyes of the horse.

"This is a kind horse, a gentle and faithful horse," Pierre said, "and I can see a beautiful spirit shining out of the eyes of the horse. I will name him after good St. Joseph, who was also kind and gentle and faithful and a beautiful spirit."

Within a year Joseph knew the milk route as well as Pierre. Pierre

---

* *cul-de-sac:* dead end

used to boast that he didn't need reins—he never touched them. Each morning Pierre arrived at the stables of the Provincale Milk Company at five o'clock. The wagon would be loaded and Joseph hitched to it. Pierre would call "*Bonjour, vieille ami,*"* as he climbed into his seat and Joseph would turn his head and the other drivers would smile and say that the horse would smile at Pierre. Then Jacques, the foreman, would say, "All right, Pierre, go on," and Pierre would call softly to Joseph, "*Avance, mon ami,*"** and this splendid combination would stalk proudly down the street.

The wagon, without any direction from Pierre, would roll three blocks down St. Catherine Street, then turn right two blocks along Roslyn Avenue; then left, for that was Prince Edward Street. The horse would stop at the first house, allow Pierre perhaps thirty seconds to get down from his seat and put a bottle of milk at the front door and would then go on, skipping two houses and stopping at the third. So down the length of the street. Then Joseph, still without any direction from Pierre, would turn around and come back along the other side. Yes, Joseph was a smart horse.

2. Could this be a hint about the "secret for two"?

Pierre would boast at the stable of Joseph's skill. "I never touch the reins. He knows just where to stop. Why, a blind man could handle my route with Joseph pulling the wagon."

So it went on for years—always the same. Pierre and Joseph both grew old together, but gradually, not suddenly. Pierre's huge walrus mustache was pure white now and Joseph didn't lift his knees so high or raise his head quite so much. Jacques, the foreman of the stables, never noticed that they were both getting old until Pierre appeared one morning carrying a heavy walking stick.

"Hey, Pierre," Jacques laughed. "Maybe you got the gout, hey?"

3. <u>Direct dialogue</u> is the exact words exchanged by story characters.

"*Mais oui,*** Jacques," Pierre said a bit uncertainly. "One grows old. One's legs get tired."

"You should teach that horse to carry the milk to the front door for you," Jacques told him. "He does everything else."

He knew every one of the forty families he served on Prince

---

* *Bonjour, vieille ami:* Good morning, old friend
** *Avance, mon ami:* Let's go, my friend.
*** *Mais oui:* Of course

Edward Street. The cooks knew that Pierre could neither read nor write, so instead of following the usual custom of leaving a note in an empty bottle if an additional quart of milk was needed they would sing out when they heard the rumble of his wagon wheels over the cobbled streets, "Bring an extra quart this morning, Pierre."

"So you have company for dinner tonight," he would call back gaily.

Pierre had a remarkable memory. When he arrived at the stable he'd always remember to tell Jacques, "The Paquins took an extra quart this morning; the Lemoines bought a pint of cream."

Jacques would note these things in a little book he always carried. Most of the drivers had to make out the weekly bills and collect the money, but Jacques, liking Pierre, had always excused him from this task. All Pierre had to do was to arrive at five in the morning, walk to his wagon, which was always in the same spot at the curb, and deliver his milk. He returned some two hours later, got down stiffly from his seat, called a cheery, "Au 'voir"* to Jacques and then limped slowly down the street.

One morning the president of the Provincale Milk Company came to inspect the early morning deliveries. Jacques pointed Pierre out to him and said: "Watch how he talks to that horse. See how the horse listens and how he turns his head toward Pierre? You know, I think those two share a secret. I have often noticed it. It is as though they both sometimes chuckle at us as they go off on their route. Pierre is a good man, Monsieur** President, but he gets old. Would it be too bold of me to suggest that he be retired and be given perhaps a small pension?" he added anxiously.

"But of course," the president laughed. "I know his record. He has been on this route now for thirty years and never once has there been a complaint. Tell him it is time he rested. His salary will go on just the same."

But Pierre refused to retire. He was panic-stricken at the thought of not driving Joseph every day. "We are two old men," he said to Jacques. "Let us wear out together. When Joseph is ready to retire—then I, too, will quit."

4. Here's another clue to the "secret"!

* Au' voir: Good-bye
** Monsieur: Mister; sir

5. Jacques is characterized as being kind. How is Jacques kind?

Jacques, who was a kind man, understood. There was something about Pierre and Joseph which made a man smile tenderly. It was as though each drew some hidden strength from the other. When Pierre was sitting in his seat, and when Joseph was hitched to the wagon, neither seemed old. But when they finished their work, then Pierre would limp down the street slowly, seeming very old indeed, and the horse's head would drop and he would walk very wearily to his stall.

6. The words *cold, pitch-dark,* and *iced wine* are examples of imagery. Words of imagery appeal to our senses.

Then one morning Jacques had dreadful news for Pierre when he arrived. It was a cold morning and still pitch-dark. The air was like iced wine that morning and the snow which had fallen during the night glistened like a million diamonds piled together.

Jacques said, "Pierre, your horse, Joseph, did not wake up this morning. He was very old, Pierre, he was twenty-five and that is like being seventy-five for a man."

"Yes," Pierre said slowly. "Yes, I am seventy-five. And I cannot see Joseph again."

"Of course you can," Jacques soothed. "He is over in his stall, looking very peaceful. Go over and see him."

Pierre took one step forward then turned. "No . . . no . . . you don't understand, Jacques."

Jacques clapped him on the shoulder. "We'll find another horse just as good as Joseph. Why, in a month you'll teach him to know your route as well as Joseph did. We'll . . ."

The look in Pierre's eyes stopped him. For years Pierre had worn a heavy cap, the peak of which came low over his eyes, keeping the bitter morning wind out of them. Now Jacques looked into Pierre's eyes and he saw something which startled him. He saw a dead, lifeless look in them. The eyes were mirroring the grief that was in Pierre's heart and his soul. It was though his heart and soul had died.

7. These events are the climax of the story. What does Pierre do? Why? What happens next?

"Take today off, Pierre," Jacques said, but already Pierre was hobbling off down the street, and had one been near one would have seen tears streaming down his cheeks and have heard half-smothered sobs. Pierre walked to the corner and stepped into the street.

There was a warning yell from the driver of a huge truck that was coming fast and there was the scream of brakes, but Pierre apparently heard neither.

Five minutes later an ambulance driver said, "He's dead. Was killed instantly."

Jacques and several of the milk-wagon drivers had arrived and they looked down at the still figure.

"I couldn't help it," the driver of the truck protested, "he walked right into my truck. He never saw it, I guess. Why, he walked into it as though he were blind."

The ambulance doctor bent down. "Blind? Of course the man was blind. See those cataracts? This man has been blind for five years." He turned to Jacques. "You say he worked for you? Didn't you know he was blind?"

"No . . . no . . ." Jacques said, softly. "None of us knew. Only one knew—a friend of his named Joseph. . . . It was a secret, I think, just between those two."

8. The <u>resolution</u> is the outcome of a story. What was the secret? Who were the "two"?

⸫ Present the Story

Contrast Chart ■ ■ ■

Share with students that in "A Secret for Two" they will meet an old man named Pierre. Recall with students that in "La Bamba," the young main character, Manuel, faced a challenge. Explain that in "A Secret for Two," the older character faces a challenge as well. Help students predict what that challenge could be. Encourage students to think about older people they know and to consider their strengths along with the challenges they might face. List students' ideas in a chart like the one shown here.

ANALYZING THE TRAITS OF OLDER PEOPLE	
Strengths	**Challenges**
Many life experiences	Might have failing health
Knowledge gained from those life experiences	Might need to earn a living, but have difficulty doing so
Appreciation for family and friends	Might need extra help doing day-to-day things

Distribute Copies of the Story ■ ■ ■

Mention to students that for this story you want them to pay special attention to the setting. Explain that the story takes places in Montreal, Canada. Point out the italicized phrases and footnotes, preparing students for some French words. The words' translations appear in the footnotes. Judging by the translations, speculate with students which language most people in Montreal probably speak. As students read, also ask them to figure out if the story takes place in the past or the present, and how they would describe the atmosphere of the setting.

Challenge: What's the "Secret"? ■ ■ ■

Finally, tell students that this story has a slight mystery. Review the book title, emphasizing the word *secret*. Encourage students to look for clues that might reveal what the secret is before they come to the end of the story.

∴ Read the Story

As students read the story together, refer to the margin notes to guide discussion.

Margin Note 1:
The location and time period of a story is the <u>setting</u>.
Where and when does this story take place?

Student Response: Montreal, Canada; in the past. Because horses do not pull wagons through the city any longer.

Further Discussion: Make sure students understand that *when* a story takes place is just as important as *where* it takes place. As students continue to read, point out the many phrases that paint a picture of Montreal. Ask students if they picture a hustling, bustling city, like New York, or a more quaint, charming town. Which words develop this setting for them?

Margin Note 2:
Could this be a hint about the "secret for two"?

Further Discussion: Mention to students that authors often include things for specific reasons. Yes, we can gather from Pierre's words that Joseph is a trusty horse. But what other information does Pierre mention? Suggest to students that a clue appears in the sentence about the "secret."

Margin Note 3:
<u>Direct dialogue</u> is the exact words exchanged by story characters.

Student Response: Let students take turns playing the roles of Pierre and Jacques as they read the direct dialogue.

Further Discussion: Point out to students that even Jacques, Pierre's boss, has noticed that Joseph is responsible for a large part of guiding Pierre's route. Also call attention to what starts the dialogue—Pierre's use of a walking stick. Speculate with students why someone might need a stick for walking.

Margin Note 4:
Here's another clue to the "secret"!

Further Discussion: The author is showing us that Pierre is a trustworthy employee. The author is showing us that Jacques is an understanding boss. Also encourage students to consider these actions as another clue to the "secret."

Margin Note 5:
Jacques is <u>characterized</u> as being kind. How is Jacques kind?

Student Response: Jacques is kind because he thinks Pierre should be ready to retire, but he understands why he chooses not to.

Further Discussion: Encourage students to read to you specific sentences that illustrate Jacques' kindness. For example:

◆ Most of the drivers had to make out the weekly bills and collect the money, but Jacques, liking Pierre, had always excused him from this task.

◆ [Jacques says to the president] "Pierre is a good man, Monsieur President, but he gets old. Would it be too bold of me to suggest that he be retired and be given perhaps a small pension?"

Margin Note 6:
The words *cold, pitch-dark,* and *iced wine* are examples of <u>imagery</u>. Words of <u>imagery</u> appeal to our senses.

Further Discussion: Invite students to read the paragraph out loud. Consider with them if these sound like happy words or sad words. How do the words change the tone of the story? What could be the "dreadful" news?

Margin Note 7:
These events are the <u>climax</u> of the story. What does Pierre do? Why? What happens next?

Student Response: Pierre hobbles down the street, crying. When he steps into the street, he is hit by a truck.

Further Discussion: Invite students to consider why Pierre would be so upset over Joseph's death. Could it be more than just the passing of a friend? Recall with students Pierre's earlier words: "When Joseph is ready to retire—then I, too, will quit." Could this be a reason for Pierre's sadness—the realization that he must now retire? Or could there be something else?

Margin Note 8:
The <u>resolution</u> is the outcome of a story. What was the secret? Who were the "two"?

Student Response: The secret was that Pierre had been blind for the past several years. The secret had been between Pierre and Joseph.

Further Discussion: Encourage students to explore how they feel about Pierre and Joseph's secret. Let students go back through the story to examine the clues the author provided about Pierre's blindness. For example:

◆ Pierre states that a "blind man could handle my route."

◆ Pierre walks with a stick, which could be to guide him as he walks.

◆ Pierre does not write out weekly bills but tells them to his boss.

◆ Upon learning about Joseph's death, Pierre says, "I cannot see Joseph again."

◆ Jacques sees a "dead, lifeless look" in Pierre's eyes.

Analyze the Story— As a Group

Affective Response ■ ■ ■

Reproduce and pass out copies of page 44, Personal Responses. Preview the questions, and remind students that a "personal response" is an individual reader's ideas and reactions to a story. After completing their sheets, encourage students to share and compare their responses. Point out to students that they can learn new insights about a story as they listen to and consider other people's responses to it.

On the chalkboard, draw an outline of a postcard, as shown below. You might have real postcards on hand to show the class. Talk with students about what

> Montreal, Canada, is a big city that also has small streets. Many people speak French. *(where)* In the Montreal of several decades ago, horse-drawn milk wagons were still around. *(when)* The city back then was a kind place, with people looking out for each other. *(atmosphere)*

makes a postcard special, concluding that a postcard shows a place on one side and tells about the place on the other. In the postcard outline on the board, prompt students to compose a postcard message that tells about the setting of "A Secret for Two." Make sure students include where, when, and atmosphere.

Literal Response ■ ■ ■

Reproduce and pass out the graphic organizer Exploring Story Setting on page 45. Help students fill in the first column of the chart as they identify the where, the when, and the atmosphere. Encourage students to complete the rest of the chart on their own, explaining how they are able to identify each element. Make sure students choose specific sentences, phrases, and words from the story that reflect their answers.

Challenge: Setting-the-Stage Outline ■ ■ ■

Share with students that they should view exploring a story as they would watching a movie. The author "sets the stage" for the story, leading up to the conflicts, the climax, and the ultimate resolution. Review with the class recent movies they've seen that they enjoyed. Ask students to explain how the movie-maker "set the stage" for the film. For example:

◆ What was the setting of the movie? Where did it take place? When? What was the atmosphere like?

◆ Which characters did the moviemaker introduce to you? What were they like?

◆ After setting the stage by establishing the story setting and introducing the characters, what problem or conflict did the moviemaker reveal?

◆ How does the action lead up to the movie's climax?

◆ How is the problem solved or the conflict resolved? In other words, what is the movie's resolution?

On the following page is an example of how to set up a Setting the Stage outline for "A Secret for Two." Work through the outline with the class. You might encourage students to apply the outline to other stories they've read or that the class will read in the future. Make sure students understand that establishing the setting is all part of "setting the stage" for a story.

Talk with students about why setting the stage for this story is important. For example, could the story have taken place in the present? On a large city street with many buildings? Make sure students understand that setting the stage for a story is just as important as deciding on an idea for a story.

Setting-the-Stage Outline

1. Set the Stage: Story Setting
   Where: _____ Montreal, Canada _____
   When: _____ In the past _____
   Atmosphere: _____ Friendly, quaint city _____

2. Set the Stage: Introduce the Main Characters
   Name: _____ Pierre _____
   Characteristics: _____ old, likes animals, hardworking, reliable ____
   Name: _____ Joseph, a horse _____
   Characteristics: _____ old, trustworthy, helpful, good friend _____
   Name: _____ Jacques _____
   Characteristics: _____ kind boss, understanding _____

3. What Is the Problem or Conflict?
   Pierre and Joseph appear to be getting too old for the milk route. ____

4. Action/Events Leading up to the Climax:
   daily routine of Pierre and Joseph _____
   clues dropped about the "secret" _____
   Joseph dies _____

5. Climax:
   Pierre is upset, and he dies when hit by a truck. _____

6. How is the Problem Solved/Conflict Resolved?
   Pierre had been blind all along, so it is only fitting that he and Joseph both pass _
   away at the same time. _____

Analyze the Story— On Their Own

Retell the Story—Plot Points ▪ ▪ ▪

To focus on plot points, invite students to:

◆ Explain the story, simply, using the one-sentence story summary format. In their summaries, make sure students include the setting, main characters, and major events or actions.

◆ Encourage students to go through the story and write down the clues that suggest to the reader that Pierre might be blind. Explain that now that they know of Pierre's blindness, these clues should be more apparent to them.

Retell the Story—Another Format ▪ ▪ ▪

◆ Encourage students to write a newspaper obituary about Pierre. Assure students that this task isn't as dismal as it sounds. Explain that obituaries usually summarize people's achievements and strengths. Preface the writing assignment by reading obituaries from local or national newspapers. Then have fun with the class as you ask them to help you write an obituary for Pierre's horse, Joseph.

> Joseph, the milk-wagon horse, passed away peacefully at the age of 25 as he slept in his warm stable. Joseph was prompt and accurate in his milk deliveries. His driver, Pierre, said of him: "This is a kind horse, a gentle and faithful horse, and I can see a beautiful spirit shining out of the eyes of this horse." Joseph will be especially remembered for the secret he shared with Pierre: Pierre had lost his eyesight, but Joseph knew the milk route by heart. Joseph was indeed "a faithful horse." He was loved by everyone along his delivery route.

After exploring examples, encourage students to compose their own obituaries for Pierre.

◆ Arrange the class into groups, and invite the groups to present talk-show segments in which a host interviews Jacques, other milk drivers, and customers along Pierre's route. Instruct the student playing the host to ask questions that begin with *who, what, when, where, why, how.* These questions will require more than simply "yes" or "no" responses, making the talk shows more lively. Encourage those students role-playing the talk-show guests to answer with information from the story as well as their own impressions and ideas.

Expand the Story ▪ ▪ ▪

To focus on setting, encourage students to:

◆ Draw and complete a chart that contrasts the setting of "A Secret for Two" with the setting for "La Bamba." On the chalkboard, set up a chart, like the one shown here.

Story	Where	When	Ethnic Community
"La Bamba"	Southern California	the present	Latino community
"A Secret for Two"	Montreal, Canada	the past	French-Canadian city

After students complete the chart, ask broad questions that help focus on the importance of setting in any story. For example:

◆ Could the story of a blind milkman and his horse be set in southern California today? Why or why not? (Possible answer: No; horses are not used today to make deliveries, trucks are.)

◆ Imagine that a student in Montreal, 75 years ago, takes part in a school talent show. Would the student choose to perform "La Bamba"? Why or why not? (Possible answer: No; the song "La Bamba" did not exist 75 years ago.)

Plan an Original Story ■ ■ ■

EXPLORING
LITERARY
ELEMENTS

Story Setting—Atmosphere Review with students that atmosphere is a key component in a story's setting. Many students will benefit from thinking about atmosphere in terms of colors and pictorial renditions. Guide students to consider atmosphere as they weave it into the fabric of a story setting. Do so by letting them create colorful murals that evoke emotions, mood, and atmosphere.

1. Introduce atmosphere by asking a volunteer to read the definition in the glossary of this book.

2. Then brainstorm with students words that describe the atmosphere of "La Bamba" and "A Secret for Two." For example:
◆ "La Bamba": *fun, exciting, suspenseful, happy*
◆ "A Secret for Two": *friendly, mysterious, loving, sad*

At this time, you might also introduce students to the term *bittersweet*. Explain that this word can describe an atmosphere that is both sad and happy. Talk about how that could describe both stories.

3. Discuss colors one could use to portray different atmospheres. Encourage students to consider the moods or feelings they associate with different colors when they create art. For example:
◆ gray, brown, pale blue: create atmospheres that are quiet, peaceful, sad, or mysterious
◆ red, yellow, orange: create atmospheres that are exciting, fun, or suspenseful

4. Divide the class into groups of four and give each a length of mural paper. Have them divide the mural paper in half, titling one side "La Bamba" and the other side "A Secret for Two." Encourage students to paint a scene from each story, primarily using colors that evoke each story's atmosphere. Speculate with students if "La Bamba" would be mostly bright or cheerful colors. What about "A Secret for Two"?

5. Review students' murals for atmosphere. Guide the discussion by relating the atmosphere to story setting. Make sure students can relate that atmosphere is part of "setting the stage" for a story, along with the location and time period.

Main Characters After setting the stage with a good setting and compelling atmosphere, encourage students to consider a character. Share with the class the glossary definitions for Character and Characterization found in this book. Encourage students to consider how the story character relates to the setting they developed.

Dialogue Dialogue is essential in developing a character's personality. Through the words a character exchanges with others or says out loud to himself or herself, we learn the character's feelings, thoughts, perhaps even their goals and motivations. To get students thinking about dialogue, encourage partners to role-play an exchange of dialogue between two story characters *from different stories.*

For example, Manuel of "La Bamba" and Pierre of "A Secret for Two" both have a secret. Manuel's performance for the talent show, along with his motivations and hopes, are a secret to those around him. Pierre's secret is his blindness. Suggest that students write dialogue between Manuel and Pierre as they discuss their secrets and the conflicts they cause. Allow students to present their dialogues as a Readers Theater presentation or in a talk-show format.

Another common theme to explore are "survival" stories. Review any survival stories and characters your class is familiar with, such as:

> Julie, from *Julie of the Wolves*
> Billy Wind, from *The Talking Earth*
> Mafatu, from *Call It Courage*
> Sam, from *My Side of the Mountain*

Encourage groups of students to choose characters from these stories and write dialogue between them. Remind students that the dialogue should reflect not only the wilderness experience but the character's personality too.

Share Your Writing ■ ■ ■

Let students review, assess, and revise their stories following the traditional Writing Partner procedure. (See the Writing Partner Conference on page 87). Or, try the following:

Reading Poll. Show students how to elicit positive comments about their stories. Working with a partner or a small group, encourage the writer to pose the following question: What part of my story do you like best? Why? As the writer listens to classmates' input, the writer should jot down notes. Upon reviewing the notes, the reader should be able to analyze where the story needs work and further revisions.

Story 2   A Secret for Two

Personal Responses

1. After reading a story, readers often come away with deep feelings for it, or an "emotional response." Describe your emotional response to this story.

_____

_____

_____

_____

_____

2. Did the ending of the story surprise you? Were you surprised to learn that Pierre was blind? Explain your answer.

_____

_____

_____

_____

_____

_____

3. In your own words, describe the relationship between Pierre and Joseph.

_____

_____

_____

_____

_____

4. In your own words, describe the setting of the story. How would you describe the atmosphere?

_____

_____

_____

_____

_____

Exploring Story Setting

Think about the setting of the story. Write your ideas about it in the chart below.

When: _____	How do you know?	Examples from the story: _____
_____	_____	_____
_____	_____	_____
_____	_____	_____
_____	_____	_____
_____	_____	_____
_____	_____	_____
_____	_____	_____
_____	_____	_____
_____	_____	_____
Where: _____	How do you know?	Examples from the story: _____
_____	_____	_____
_____	_____	_____
_____	_____	_____
_____	_____	_____
_____	_____	_____
_____	_____	_____
_____	_____	_____
_____	_____	_____
Atmosphere: _____	How do you know?	Examples from the story: _____
_____	_____	_____
_____	_____	_____
_____	_____	_____
_____	_____	_____
_____	_____	_____
_____	_____	_____
_____	_____	_____

Developing Story Settings

Fill in the chart below to create a story character of your own.

Think about a setting in which you'd like to set a story. Write notes about the story setting below.

1. **Place.** In which country or community will your story take place?

_____

What words could describe this place? _____

_____

_____

2. **Time.** During which time period will your story take place? It could be in the past, the present, or even in the future. _____

_____

What words could describe this time period? _____

_____

_____

_____

3. **Atmosphere.** What is your story setting like? Is it a cheerful setting? A scary setting? A busy setting? _____

_____

What other words could describe this atmosphere? _____

_____

_____

_____

4. **Rough Draft.** Write a descriptive paragraph about your setting, designed to "hook" the readers by getting them interested in the setting. Use the other side of this page if you run out of room. _____

_____

_____

_____

_____

Symbols, Similes, and Metaphors

Recognizing the symbols, similes, and metaphors in a story adds depth not only to the plot, but to the author's purpose in writing a story. To help students discover and explore the literary elements like symbolism, similes, and metaphors invite them to read "How Many Stars in My Crown?" by Rosemary Wells, from her book *Mary on Horseback: Three Mountain Stories*.

Story Summary ■ ■ ■

Set in the Appalachian Mountains in 1932, this story is told from the first-person point of view of Pearl, a young girl who has suffered the death of her mother. Her mother died while giving birth to twins, Pearl's new brother and sister. Pearl hasn't spoken a word since her mother's death. Feeling he has nowhere to turn, Pearl's father leaves Pearl and the newborns at a hospital. While there, Pearl meets a woman named Mary, who is recovering from an accident. Through Mary's gentle prodding, Pearl not only speaks again but helps others as well.

Literary Elements—Symbols , Similes, and Metaphors ■ ■ ■

As students appreciate Pearl's story, they will explore the following literary elements:

◆ **Symbols.** A symbol is anything that represents an idea.

◆ **Similes.** These are descriptions that compare one thing to another, using the words *like* or *as*, that help the reader to better imagine something.

◆ **Metaphors.** Metaphors are also comparisons, but they do not use the words *like* or *as*.

How Many Stars in My Crown?

by Rosemary Wells

from *Mary on Horseback: Three Mountain Stories*

The twins were born May 4, 1932. Mamma went down with childbed fever soon after. Pa got her the preacher. The preacher said he intended to breathe the breath of the Lord into her lungs because of the two little babies needin' their mamma. That left me entirely out of the picture, but it wasn't any use to say, "What about me?" Mamma was too far gone for the breath of the Lord.

I patted her hot hand, and I said over and over, "Mamma, don't leave me. Don't die. Can you hear me? It's your ownliest sugarplum talking. It's Pearl. Can you hear me?"

The preacher told me to sit quiet and not to get in the Lord's way. Just before Mamma left this earth on her way to heaven, I felt all her last strength drain into my hand. Then her spirit went on up through the open window into the night. I watched out the window and thought I saw her move across the sky and say good-bye, but I'm not sure it wasn't a cloud.

I looked up when the preacher was gone, and my pa was in the corner of the room in the dark. That's where we stayed with Mamma until morning. Since then I have not spoken a single word.

1. Pearl is the <u>main character</u>. Why do you suppose Pearl hasn't spoken since her mother died?

2. Pearl's father is faced with a prob-lem. What do you think his solution will be?

The twins hardly ate after Mamma died. My pa'll be the first to tell you he doesn't know one thing about babies. He wanted to lean on me to keep the twins alive. He couldn't do that, and he knew it.

So Pa drank three cups of coffee in a row and told me the twins were going to die if we didn't get them down to that new hospital at Hyden. That's more than a two-day ride straight downhill.

Pa said, "I'm clean out of cash money. Not a red cent, so we'll take the cow for payment."

We made our way down the mountain along Hell-fer-Sartin Creek—Pa in the saddle holding Eva, and me on the mule's rump hold-ing Ben. Those babies didn't even cry anymore. At night Pa built a fire and we warmed the twins up. I milked the cow and soaked the corner of a handkerchief in the milk. I tried to get them to suck on it, but they wouldn't take but a dib.

We wrapped them together like two little hurt sparrows in their blanket. They were still breathing in and out, but that's about all.

Late the next morning we came to the hospital. Pa didn't say a word, he just handed Eva over to a nurse. She took Ben too.

3. Pa's speech tells us about his character. What do you think about Pa? about his deci-sion?

"Keep the cow please, ma'am, in payment," said Pa. I was holding the cow's rope. "This here's Pearl. I want her to stay on and learn how to raise up these babies. Pearl is a real good girl and will earn her keep. She ain't said a word since her mamma died, but she ought to come around soon." Pa gave me a little smile. "I'll fetch you home by first frost."

Pa turned the mule's head up the path and clucked to her to get on.

"Won't you speak, little girl? What's your name?" the nurses asked me. I shook my head and did not answer their questions, so they stopped asking. All the same, I liked those nurses in their blue coats. I could not keep my eyes off them. They moved like beautiful angels from the Garden of Paradise.

Each morning I sat on the steps of the hospital and watched every little thing going on. I picked wildflowers and made daisy chains and crowns of butter and eggs.* The third morning a lady wheeled herself up in a wheelchair. "My name is Mary Breckinridge," she said. "I'm pleased to meet you."

I didn't answer.

"Nurse Texas told me about you, Pearl. You lost your mother. Is that right?"

No answer from me, but here was the first person on earth who knew I lost Mamma as well as Eva and Ben losing her. Right then I almost told Mary Breckinridge what would happen if I even spoke one word. I might cry forever and ever. I didn't want to do that kind of crying.

4. Mary's words tell us about her <u>character</u>. How would you describe Mary?

I followed her into the building. "Here I am in this wheelchair because I broke my back falling off a horse. After eight years in the saddle riding in these mountains—can you imagine that?" she asked. "But I'll be on my feet in no time. Meanwhile you can help me. I've got six hospital clinics, twenty-two nurses, and five couriers to direct and take care of and pay for and see it all works perfectly. How about that?"

She had a pile of mail as big as the post office at Hell-fer-Sartin. She let me lick the stamps for her envelopes. "Pearl," she said, "you don't have to say a blessed word if you don't want to. Too many people talk my ear off anyway."

In my lap was a daisy chain.

"Put that lovely flower garland around my neck, Pearl," said Mary Breckinridge. "It'll cheer up my whole day." She gave me more stamps to lick and set me sorting paper clips and elastic bands. I got 'em all in straight lines for her.

5. What might the "crown of buttercups and wild roses" <u>symbolize</u> in this story?

Next morning I waited for Mary again. I made her a crown of buttercups and wild roses. She put it right on her head. "Now I'm the Queen of the Wheelchair Brigade, Pearl," she said, and we were back at work.

"You've never seen a telephone, have you, child?" said Mary.

* butter and eggs: This refers to the color of the flowers in the crowns Pearl makes.

I shook my head, I watched her talk on it. Was she talking to the wind?

I eat with the nurses. Because I don't speak, they talk in front of me as if I am deaf too. I hear about Ben and Eva. It will be Christmas before they can go home, said one. Holding their own all the same, said another. In the evenings Nurse Peacock and Nurse Ireland play cards with me, double solitaire and hearts. They bet pennies on gin rummy, and they let me use bottle caps.

I sleep upstairs in the children's ward. Mostly it's quiet, but one night I heard Mary's wheelchair. Then I heard screams. I crept down the corridor and watched. The nurses were caring for a little girl. I could hardly look at her. She was burned all over.

The next morning Mary told me to give my buttercup necklace to the little burned girl, Lily. I put it right where she could see it. Two eyes peered out of the bandages, blinked at the flowers, and looked at me.

After three days Lily said something. I couldn't understand because of the bandages across her mouth. She said it again. It was water she wanted. I put a glass straw through her lips.

I could not talk to Lily, but I could hum. "How Many Stars Will There Be in My Crown?" That's my favorite song. Then I brought out a deck of cards and dealt out hearts, me playing for both of us. Her feet were unburned and I bathed them in cool water. I combed what there was of her hair. She liked it. I could tell.

After six days Lily's bed was suddenly empty. I looked everywhere for her. Finally I went into Mary's office.

"Lily has died, Pearl," Mary said. She watched me carefully. I made only little sounds like a kitten mewing. The clock ticked away time until Mary took out a shoe box full of photographs of children. She set them out on her desk like solitaire cards.

"Come and look, Pearl," she said, and picked up two of the pictures.

"This is my son, Breckie, and my daughter, Polly, when she was

51

just born. They both died when they were so young. For a while I wanted to follow them to heaven. But instead I studied to be a nurse."

Mary fanned out the rest of the pictures. "After the Great War they sent us American nurses to France because thousands of children needed help. The boys and girls in these pictures are the ones we saved. I know each one by name."

I edged over to Mary's shoulder and we looked at all the pictures and she read out the funny snurled-up names from that far-off land of France.

We listened to the clock again for a while. Then we put away the pictures. "There's not much the doctor could do for Lily. I've seen a dozen little girls burned because their dresses catch fire from the cooking stoves. Little boys are safer. They wear overalls."

Mary typed out a letter. I couldn't read it, but she told me what it said. It was to a factory asking them to give us a couple of crates of children's overalls for her to pass out to mountain families so there'll be no more little girls on fire.

I put the stamp on nice and straight.

One day Mary left. She was going to Lexington, she said, to have her back brace taken off so she could ride again. "Hold the fort, Pearl," Mary said.

She was gone a whole week. I rolled pennies and cleaned out every single letter of her typewriter keys with Bon Ami on a toothbrush. I sharpened the pencils and sorted the little hickies in the china dish over the mantel.

Mary came home walking. The wheelchair was gone. She brought with her two big boxes. In them were a hundred pair of overalls all little sizes. Every nurse got some to hand out.

At first Mary could only ride for a little bit, but at the end of the summer she said, "I'm good as store-bought now, Pearl. Are you coming with me?"

I got a donkey called Coolidge. We went up Hurricane Creek

where there's lots of cabins. At each one Mary said, "Good afternoon, ma'am. I'm from the Frontier Nursing Service. Do you have a little girl and does she tend the cooking fire for you?" Mary went into every cabin while I held her horse and Coolidge.

At the last cabin of the day Mary saw a little girl. "Size four, Pearl," she said. "I'm too sore and tired to get off and on another time. Square up your shoulders, hold your head high, and speak out!"

I didn't even think to refuse Mary.

"Good afternoon, ma'am," said I at the cabin door. "I'm from the Frontier Nurses. Does your little girl yonder tend your cooking fire?"

We went home along the creek-bed in the twilight. Me on my donkey, Mary on horseback.

7. These events are the climax of the story. Is Pearl finally going to speak?

8. The resolution is the outcome of a story. What does Pearl resolve? How do you think she feels?

Present the Story

Story Background ▪ ▪ ▪

Share a bit with students about the background of this story. Explain that the story they are about to read is based on an incident in the life of Mary Breckinridge (1881–1965). Mary Breckinridge was a nurse who survived the death of her husband and two children as well as service as a nurse in France during World War I. In 1923, Breckinridge went to the isolated Appalachian Mountains of Kentucky to establish the Frontier Nursing Service. Along with three other nurses, Breckinridge traveled on horseback through the mountain wilderness to find and assist families who needed medical help. By 1931, more than thirty nurses and couriers had joined Breckinridge, and she had established six outpost clinics and a 40-bed hospital. Today, Frontier Nursing visits about 35,000 mountain homes each year. Explain that although this story is mostly about a young girl named Pearl, students should look for Mary in the story too.

A "Feelings" Web ▪ ▪ ▪

Remind students that analyzing a story character's emotions is extremely important when trying to understand that story character. Draw the following word web on the chalkboard. Explain that each of these feelings—sadness, fear, and usefulness—are feelings that the main character in this story experiences. Mention to students that the character lives in the Appalachian Mountains, and she will be helped by Mary Breckinridge. Discuss incidents for each emotion in the web, letting students share their own experiences if they so wish.

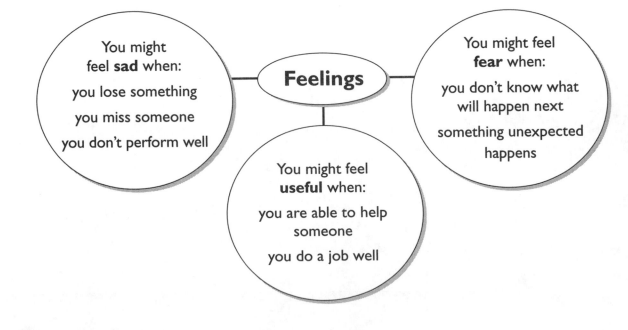

You might feel **sad** when:

you lose something

you miss someone

you don't perform well

Feelings

You might feel **fear** when:

you don't know what will happen next

something unexpected happens

You might feel **useful** when:

you are able to help someone

you do a job well

Distribute Copies of the Story ■ ■ ■

As you pass out copies of the story, explain that this story is a bit different from "La Bamba" and "A Secret for Two." Ask students if they remember who told each story. Confirm that the stories were told in the **third person**. That means, they were told by a narrator who knew everything, yet was not part of the action. "How Many Stars in My Crown?" is told in the **first person**. That means that someone in the story tells what happens, using the word *I*. Tell students that they will learn who the first-person narrator is at the beginning of the story.

Look for Symbolism, Similes, and Metaphors ■ ■ ■

Review the story title with the class. Tell students that the "crown" and "stars" are symbols that represent something important. Encourage students to look for these references, mentioning that the notes in the margin will help them. Invite them to note any similes and metaphors they encounter.

Read the Story

As students read the story together, refer to the margin notes to guide discussion.

Margin Note 1:

Pearl is the <u>main character</u>. Why do you suppose Pearl hasn't spoken since her mother died?

Student Response: She is sad because her mother died. She is afraid of the future.

Further Discussion: Point out to students that the author has chosen to tell Pearl's story from Pearl herself, which is a good strategy since Pearl does not speak. Predict with students what might cause Pearl to speak again.

Margin Note 2:

Pearl's father is faced with a <u>problem.</u>
What do you think his <u>solution</u> will be?

Student Response: Pa's problem is keeping the twins alive. He might do this by calling a doctor, taking the twins to a hospital, asking a neighbor for help, sending Pearl off to get help, and so on.

Further Discussion: Remind students that identifying the problem helps us understand why characters may react as they do. For example, Pa must do something to solve the problem of the ailing babies. His solution might affect

Pearl's life.

Margin Note 3:
Pa's speech tells us about his <u>character</u>. What do you think about Pa? About his decision?

Student Response: Pa is not a wealthy man because he has no money to pay for the babies' medical care. But he is polite, and he knows his duties and responsibilities. Pa's decision to leave Pearl is probably a difficult one, but is a wise choice.

Further Discussion: Point out the use of the word *ain't*. Remind students that this word is not correct English grammar. Explain that this is not a mistake. The author included it to demonstrate Pa's lack of a proper education.

Margin Note 4:
Mary's words tell us about her <u>character</u>. How would you describe Mary?

Student Response: Mary appears friendly and outgoing. She doesn't mind sharing details about her life. She is optimistic about her recovery and is full of energy.

Further Discussion: Help students realize that in Mary's short speech, we learn a lot about her. We learn that she's been riding horseback through the mountains for eight years. We also learn about her clinics. Recall with students the information you shared with them about Mary Breckinridge before reading.

Margin Note 5:
What might the "crown of buttercups and wild roses" <u>symbolize</u> in this story?

Student Response: The crown could symbolize Pearl's way of communicating her feelings, even though she has not spoken.

Further Discussion: Share with students that the crown's meaning might not be apparent yet. But each time they read about Pearl's crowns of flowers, the symbolism will reveal itself.

Margin Note 6:
What is Mary's <u>motivation</u> for sharing her story with Pearl?

Student Response: Mary is trying to help Pearl. She is trying to show Pearl that life goes on, and we can learn from personal tragedy and be useful to others in need.

Further Discussion: Point out that Mary's personal tragedy motivated her to help other boys and girls. Speculate with students if they think Mary's idea to share her past with Pearl will make Pearl speak again.

Margin Note 7:

These events are the <u>climax</u> of the story.
Is Pearl finally going to speak?

Student Response: Student responses will vary, but most students should realize by now that Mary's willingness to help others has an impact on Pearl, and yes, Pearl will speak.

Further Discussion: As you discuss this moment in the story, point out Pearl's conflict: She has chosen not to speak, yet Mary has asked for her help. Pearl must resolve this inner conflict in order for the story to reach its resolution.

Margin Note 8:

The <u>resolution</u> is the outcome of a story. What does Pearl
resolve? How do you think she feels?

Student Response: Pearl finally speaks. She probably feels relieved, a bit anxious, proud to be with Mary, useful, and ultimately happy.

Further Discussion: Talk with the class in more detail about Pearl's decision to speak again. Do they think Mary was really too tired to speak to the young girl? Did they think Pearl would refuse Mary's request?

Analyze the Story— As a Group

Affective Response ■ ■ ■

SHARING RESPONSES

Reproduce and pass out copies of page 62, Personal Responses. As students consider and write down their answers, encourage them to keep in mind that Pearl is not their contemporary. She lived more than 50 years ago. Her home life and living conditions, as well as the circumstances that bring her to the hospital and Mary Breckinridge, may be unfamiliar to them. Suggest that the unfamiliar circumstances of Mary's life is what makes reading the story so fascinating—glimpsing lives other than their own. Encourage students to share their responses to the story.

On the chalkboard, draw an outline of a crown with stars. Or invite a student

EXPLORING LITERARY ELEMENTS

volunteer to do so. Make sure the stars of the crown are large enough to write in. You might also do this ahead of time, drawing the crown on a large sheet of poster paper. Let students exchange ideas about what the "stars" in Pearl's crown could be, and write their ideas in the stars. If time and interest allows, you might do the same for Mary Breckinridge. Below are possible answers for Pearl.

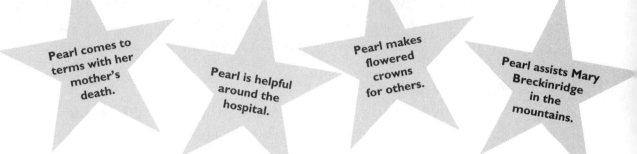

Pearl comes to terms with her mother's death.

Pearl is helpful around the hospital.

Pearl makes flowered crowns for others.

Pearl assists Mary Breckinridge in the mountains.

Literal Response ■ ■ ■

Write the words *simile metaphor* on the chalkboard, and elicit from students what they mean. Reproduce and pass out copies of page 63. Invite volunteers to read each description in the left-hand column, identify it as either a simile or metaphor, and then explain the object being described and what it is being compared to. Discuss why the simile or metaphor is a good description. Encourage students to fill out the sheet with their own ideas.

Challenge: Focus on Symbolism ■ ■ ■

Remind students that this story is titled "How Many Stars in My Crown?" Point out that images and descriptions of necklaces and crowns of flowers appear several times in the story. Write the following examples from the story on the chalkboard:

◆ I picked wildflowers and made daisy chains and crowns of butter and eggs.

◆ "Put that lovely flower garland round my neck, Pearl," said Mary Breckinridge.

◆ I made her a crown of buttercups and wild roses.

◆ I could not talk to Lily, but I could hum. "How Many Stars Will There Be in My Crown?" That's my favorite song.

A great way for students to explore a story is by exploring it along with you. Students can always profit when you become a co-reader, sharing with them your own heartfelt reactions. For this story, model a think-aloud procedure to demonstrate how you explore a recurring symbol. Refer to the examples from the book that you wrote on the chalkboard. Below are comments about each to guide your discussion.

Reference 1 To me, crowns and flowers and necklaces stand for, or *symbolize*, happiness. At first, I wondered: So why does Pearl, who's sad and grieving for her mother, make these happy things? Then I concluded that maybe she creates them to keep busy and to make something beautiful. What were your first ideas about the flower crowns and necklaces? (Accept a wide variety of ideas.)

Reference 2 As I read further, I realize that Pearl usually gives her flower crowns and necklaces to others. I asked myself: To whom do I like to give beautiful things that I've made? What would your answer be? (Answers will vary, but will probably focus on people students like or admire.)

Reference 3 I came to realize that Pearl's garlands and crowns symbolize, or stand for, love and caring. Pearl loved her mother. In the story, who else does Pearl come to love and care for? (The twin babies, Lily, Mary Breckinridge)

Reference 4 After I finished reading the story, the title made sense to me. Not only is "How Many Stars Will There Be in My Crown?" the name of Pearl's favorite song, but the "crown" reminds me of the flower crowns Pearl makes.

Analyze the Story— On Their Own

Retell the Story—Plot Points ▪ ▪ ▪

To focus on plot, invite students to:

◆ Explain the story, simply, using the one-sentence story summary format. In their summaries, make sure students include the setting, main characters, and the conflict/problem within Pearl, as well as how it is resolved.

◆ Invite students to retell the story as they explain the symbolism. As they do so, students should mention the loss of Pearl's mother and how Mary helped Pearl, relating the events to the "stars" in Pearl's "crown."

Retell the Story—Another Format ▪ ▪ ▪

◆ To focus on first-person point of view, encourage students to work with partners to plan, script, and present a readers theater summary of the story. Instruct students to choose two characters, other than Pearl, to hold a conversation. For example, Mary Breckinridge and Pearl's father could tell about their experiences and feelings about losing loved ones, specifically, children. Or Mary and another nurse at the hospital could discuss Pearl, her refusal to speak, and possible solutions. Below is an example to present to the class. Invite two volunteers to each take a part.

Pearl's Father: When my wife died, I just didn't know how to take care of the babies. I felt I had to rely on Pearl.

Mary: That's a big burden for a young girl. Pearl couldn't even talk after her mother died.

Pearl's Father: I realize that now. Did Pearl do okay at the clinic?

Mary: Absolutely! Pearl became a clinic superstar!

Pearl's Father: Good for Pearl! Tell me what happened.

Point out to students the familiar language of the dialogue, stressing to partners that their scripts should use natural language as well.

Expand the Story ■ ■ ■

To focus on plot, character, and conflict, encourage students to:

◆ Choose a future situation for Pearl and write a story about it. For example, Pearl returns home with the twins, then tells her father that she is going back to the hospital to live and help the nurses. Or Mary Breckinridge realizes that her hospitals need money for supplies. Pearl searches for ways to raise money.

◆ Think of another young girl or boy that Mary Breckinridge could help. Have them consider a problem that a boy or girl might face in the Appalachian Mountains. If possible, suggest that students research a bit about the area. Challenge students to write a story that focuses on the problem, how Mary and Pearl help, and the ultimate solution or resolution of the story.

Plan an Original Story ■ ■ ■

Story Setting Remind students that the setting of "How Many Stars in My Crown?"—the location and the time period—are essential literary elements. The setting here builds background for Pearl as well as moves the story forward when Mary ventures into the mountains to help others. Encourage students to develop story setting, using the sheet on page 46.

Story Characters Briefly discuss and review with students how Mary helped

Pearl get through a terribly difficult time in her life. Encourage students to consider problems children in their community might face. So the activity does not become personal, make sure students understand that their characters should not be based on real people but on possible situations. Reproduce and pass out page 64 for students to complete about their character.

Point of View Recall with students that Pearl's story is told in the first person. That is, it is told from Pearl's point of view. Invite students to try writing from this point of view, telling the story as if they are the main character. Suggest to students that as they write, they are "acting" the role of the main character.

Problem-Solver Suggest to students that Mary Breckinridge is a "problem-solver." She sees the problems many people in the Appalachian Mountains face, and she strives to solve them. Using Mary as an example, encourage students to find out about the achievements of older people in their own families, extended families, or neighborhoods. Suggest that these people could be the basis for the problem-solver character of their stories. As students interview these models, encourage them to take notes or to tape-record the responses (with permission).

Symbolism Recall with students that the crowns of flowers Pearl creates are symbols throughout the story. Challenge students to think of an object or objects that could be symbolic in their stories. Ask students, "What does the symbol stand for? Why is it important to the story?"

Share Your Writing ▪ ▪ ▪

Let students review, assess, and revise their stories following the Writing Partner procedure. (See the reproducible on page 87). Or try the following:

Ask for Help. Before reading a story draft to a group of classmates, instruct a writer to decide which part of the story she or he feels needs further work. Maybe it's an unnatural flow of dialogue, or a gap in the plot, or a problem in establishing the conflict, or trouble describing the setting. Before reading the draft, tell the writer to present the problem to the class audience. For example:

> I want to show that Ben loves his mom, but that he can't find a way to express that love. Please help me here. Listen to my story, and then make some suggestions about how Ben might show his mother how much he loves her.

Explain to writers that while they should value the input of the audience, they need not use all—or even any—of the suggestions. Writers will find that simply presenting the problem and listening to audience feedback often helps them come up with a unique solution of their own.

Personal Responses

1. After reading a story, readers often come away with deep feelings for it, or an "emotional response." Describe your emotional response to this story.

_____

_____

_____

_____

_____

2. After reading the story, what does the story title mean to you? What is the "crown"? What are the "stars"?

_____

_____

_____

_____

_____

3. Pearl chooses to take care of Lily, the burn victim. Why do you suppose she chooses this sad and difficult task?

_____

_____

_____

_____

_____

4. In what ways are Pearl and Mary alike? Why do you think Mary and Pearl are drawn to each other?

_____

_____

_____

_____

_____

Understanding Similes and Metaphors

A simile is a way to describe something by comparing it to something else.
The comparison is made using the words *like* or *as*. A metaphor is a comparison
that does not use the words *like* or *as*. Read each simile or metaphor in the first
column, and discuss it in the second column.

Similes or Metaphors	When I read this simile or metaphor, I imagine/I understand that . . .
1. We wrapped them together **like two little hurt sparrows in their blanket.**	
2. "Too many people **talk my ear off** anyway."	
3. I made only little sounds **like a kitten mewing.**	
4. "I'm **as good as store-bought now, Pearl . . ."**	

Practicing Characterization

Develop a character for your own story. Follow the steps below.

1. **The Basics.** First, write down some basic information about your character:

Character's Name: _____ Age: _____

Character's Goal: _____

Character's Problem/Conflict in Achieving Goal: _____

_____

2. **Direct Characterization.** Describe what your character is like. What do most people "see" when they first meet the character? Include physical appearance and obvious personality traits. _____

_____

_____

_____

_____

_____

_____

3. **Indirect Characterization.** What is your character like that people *can't* see? What is not obvious to the reader and other characters in the story? These indirect qualities add a bit of mystery to your character and give your character more depth. Write a few sentences about it. _____

_____

_____

_____

_____

_____

4. **Dialogue.** Write a few things your character might say to others that describe his or her personality. _____

_____

_____

_____

_____

Plot

The plot, of course, is the story itself. It is the "meat and potatoes" of a tale, the substance. In many cases, it is the first story element that readers are aware of, for the plot involves the main idea. But it is more than that. It is the sequence of story events, the problem that must be solved, and it is the climax and the resolution. To help students investigate plot and the literary elements involved, share with them the "The Circuit" by Francisco Jimenez.

Story Summary ▪ ▪ ▪

Panchito is a child in a Mexican family of migrant workers. His family makes its living traveling around California to tend and harvest various crops when they are in season. Once the grueling work is complete and the crop has been harvested, it is time for the family to move on to the next crop. This cycle, or "circuit," repeats throughout the year. While Panchito loves his close, warm family, he longs for a permanent home. One fall, Panchito enrolls in the local elementary school. A teacher, Mr. Lema, understands Panchito's situation, and he also uncovers the boy's musical talent. Happy with his new school, Panchito goes home to find his family once again packing.

Literary Elements—Plot ▪ ▪ ▪

As students appreciate Panchito's story, they will explore literary elements that help develop plot.

◆ **Main Idea.** This is what the story is mostly about.

◆ **Complication.** The complication is a problem or a conflict that the main character must face and come to terms with.

◆ **Sequence.** These are the events, in order, that move the story along.

◆ **Climax.** This is the point in the story that the sequence of events has been building up to.

The Circuit

by Francisco Jimenez

1. What is the story setting? What do you think a sharecropper is?

2. The mood is the feelings you get from the descriptive words and the characters' actions. What is the mood at this point in the story?

It was that time of year again. Ito, the strawberry sharecropper, did not smile. It was natural. The peak of the strawberry season was over and the last few days the workers, most of them *braceros,** were not picking as many boxes as they had during the months of June and July.

As the last days of August disappeared, so did the number of braceros. Sunday, only one—the best picker—came to work. I liked him. Sometimes we talked during our half-hour lunch break. That is how I found out he was from Jalisco, the same state in Mexico my family was from. That Sunday was the last time I saw him.

When the sun had tired and sunk behind the mountains, Ito signaled us that it was time to go home. "*Ya esora,*"** he yelled in his broken Spanish. Those were the words I waited for twelve hours a day, every day, seven days a week, week after week. And the thought of not hearing them again saddened me.

As we drove home Papá did not say a word. With both hands on the wheel, he stared at the dirt road. My older brother, Roberto, was also silent. He leaned his head back and closed his eyes. Once in a while he cleared from his throat the dust that blew in from outside.

Yes, it was that time of year. When I opened the front door to the shack, I stopped. Everything we owned was neatly packed in cardboard boxes. Suddenly I felt even more the weight of hours, days, weeks, and months of work. I sat down on a box. The thought of having to move to

---

* *braceros:* workers; manual laborers
** *Ya esora:* Ito is probably mispronouncing *es hora,* which means "It's time."

3. The "neatly packed card-board boxes" symbolize something to Panchito. What might it be?

4. This paragraph characterizes Papá. After reading this paragraph, how would you describe Papá?

5. What do you think the *olla* symbolizes to Mama?

Fresno and knowing what was in store for me there brought tears to my eyes.

That night I could not sleep. I lay in bed thinking about how much I hated this move.

A little before five o'clock in the morning, Papá woke everyone up. A few minutes later, the yelling and screaming of my little brothers and sisters, for whom the move was a great adventure, broke the silence of dawn. Shortly, the barking of the dogs accompanied them.

While we packed the breakfast dishes, Papá went outside to start the "Carcanchita." That was the name Papá gave his old '38 black Plymouth. He bought it in a used-car lot in Santa Rosa in the winter of 1949. Papá was very proud of his little jalopy. He had a right to be proud of it. He spent a lot of time looking at other cars before buying this one. When he finally chose the "Carcanchita," he checked it thoroughly before driving it out of the car lot. He examined every inch of the car. He listened to the motor, tilting his head from side to side like a parrot, trying to detect any noises that spelled car trouble. After being satisfied with the looks and sounds of the car, Papá then insisted on knowing who the original owner was. He never did find out from the car salesman, but he bought the car anyway. Papá figured the original owner must have been an important man because behind the rear seat of the car he found a blue necktie.

Papá parked the car out in front and left the motor running. "*Listo*,"* he yelled. Without saying a word, Roberto and I began to carry the boxes out to the car. Roberto carried the two big boxes and I carried the two smaller ones. Papá then threw the mattress on top of the car roof and tied it with ropes to the front and rear bumpers.

Everything was packed except Mamá's pot. It was an old large galvanized pot she had picked up at an army surplus store in Santa Maria the year I was born. The pot had many dents and nicks, and the more dents and nicks it acquired the more Mamá liked it. "*Mi olla*,"* she used to say proudly.

I held the front door open as Mamá carefully carried out her pot by both handles, making sure not to spill the cooked beans. When she got to the car, Papá reached out to help her with it. Roberto opened the

* *Listo:* Ready.
** *Mi olla:* My pot.

rear car door and Papá gently placed it on the floor behind the front seat. All of us then climbed in. Papá sighed, wiped the sweat off his forehead with his sleeve, and said wearily: "*Es todo.*"*

As we drove away, I felt a lump in my throat. I turned around and looked at our little shack for the last time.

At sunset we drove into a labor camp near Fresno. Since Papá did not speak English, Mamá asked the camp foreman if he needed anymore workers. "We don't need no more," said the foreman, scratching his head. "Check with Sullivan down the road. Can't miss him. He lives in a big white house with a fence around it."

When we got there, Mamá walked up to the house. She went through a white gate, past a row of rose bushes, up the stairs to the front door. She rang the doorbell. The porch light went on and a tall husky man came out. They exchanged a few words. After the man went in, Mamá clasped her hands and hurried back to the car. "We have work! Mr. Sullivan said we can stay there the whole season," she said, gasping and pointing to an old garage near the stables.

The garage was worn out by the years. It had no windows. The walls, eaten by termites, strained to support the roof full of holes. The dirt floor, populated by earthworms, looked like a gray road map.

That night, by the light of a kerosene lamp, we unpacked and cleaned our new home. Roberto swept way the loose dirt, leaving the hard ground. Papá plugged the holes in the walls with old newspapers and tin can tops. Mamá fed my little brothers and sisters. Papá and Roberto then brought in the mattress and placed it on the far corner of the garage. "Mamá, you and the little ones sleep on the mattress. Roberto, Panchito, and I will sleep outside under the trees," Papá said.

Early next morning Mr. Sullivan showed us where his crop was, and after breakfast, Papá, Roberto, and I headed for the vineyard to pick.

Around nine o'clock the temperature had risen to almost one hundred degrees. I was completely soaked in sweat and my mouth felt as if I had been chewing on a handkerchief. I walked over to the end of the row, picked up the jug of water we had brought, and began drinking. "Don't drink too much; you'll get sick," Roberto shouted. No sooner had he said that then I felt sick to my stomach. I dropped to my knees

6. What words could you use to describe the <u>setting</u> of this paragraph?

* *Es todo:* That's everything.

and let the jug roll off my hands. I remained motionless with my eyes glued on the hot sandy ground. All I could hear was the drone of insects. Slowly I began to recover. I poured water over my face and neck and watched the dirty water run down my arms to the ground.

I still felt a little dizzy when we took a break to eat lunch. It was past two o'clock and we sat underneath a large walnut tree that was on the side of the road. While we ate, Papá jotted down the number of boxes we had picked. Roberto drew designs on the ground with a stick. Suddenly I noticed Papá's face turn pale as he looked down the road. "Here comes the school bus," he whispered loudly in alarm. Instinctively, Roberto and I ran and hid in the vineyards. We did not want to get in trouble for not going to school. The neatly dressed boys about my age got off. They carried books under their arms. After they crossed the street, the bus drove away. Roberto and I came out from hiding and joined Papá. "*Tienen que tener cuidado,*"* he warned us.

After lunch we went back to work. The sun kept beating down. The buzzing insects, the wet sweat, and the hot dry dust made the afternoon seem to last forever. Finally the mountains around the valley reached out and swallowed the sun. Within an hour it was too dark to continue picking. The vines blanketed the grapes, making it difficult to see the bunches. "*Vámanos,*"** said Papá, signaling to us that it was time to quit work. Papá then took out a pencil and began to figure out how much we had earned our first day. He wrote down numbers, crossed some out, wrote down some more. "*Quince,*"*** he murmured.

When we arrived home, we took a cold shower under a water-hose. We then sat down to eat dinner around some wooden crates that served as a table. Mamá had cooked a special meal for us. We had rice and tortillas with "*carne con chile,*"**** my favorite dish.

The next morning I could hardly move. My body ached all over. I felt little control over my arms and legs. This feeling went on every morning for days until my muscles finally got used to the work.

It was Monday, the first week of November. The grape season was over and I could now go to school. I woke up early that morning and lay in bed, looking at the stars and savoring the thought of not going to work and of starting sixth grade for the first time that year. Since I could not sleep, I decided to get up and join Papá and Roberto at breakfast. I

* *Tienen que tener cuidado:* It's important to be careful.
** *Vamanos:* Let's go.

*** *Quince:* fifteen
**** *carne con chile:* meat with chile

7. Panchito has mixed feelings about going to school. This is an inner conflict. Why is he happy to go to school? Why does he hide his happiness?

sat at the table across from Roberto, but I kept my head down. I did not want to look up and face him. I knew he was sad. He was not going to school today. He was not going tomorrow, or next week, or next month. He would not go until the cotton season was over, and that was sometime in February. I rubbed my hands together and watched the dry, acid-stained skin fall to the floor in little rolls.

When Papá and Roberto left for work, I felt relief. I walked to the top of a small grade next to the shack and watched the "Caranchita" disappear in the distance in a cloud of dust.

Two hours later, around eight o'clock, I stood by the side of the road waiting for school bus number twenty. When it arrived I climbed in. Everyone was busy either talking or yelling. I sat in an empty seat in the back.

When the bus stopped in front of the school, I felt very nervous. I looked out the bus window and saw boys and girls carrying books under their arms. I put my hands in my pant pockets and walked to the principal's office. When I entered I heard a woman's voice say: "May I help you?" I was startled. I had not heard English for months. For a few seconds I remained speechless. I looked at the lady who waited for an answer. My first instinct was to answer her in Spanish, but I held back. Finally, after struggling for English words, I managed to tell her that I wanted to enroll in the sixth grade. After answering many questions, I was led to the classroom.

Mr. Lema, the sixth grade teacher, greeted me and assigned me a desk. He then introduced me to the class. I was so nervous and scared at that moment when everyone's eyes were on me that I wished I were with Papá and Roberto picking cotton. After taking roll, Mr. Lema gave the class the assignment for the first hour. "The first thing we have to do this morning is finish reading the story we began yesterday," he said enthusiastically. He walked up to me, handed me an English book, and asked me to read. "We are on page 125," he said politely. When I heard this, I felt my blood rush to my head; I felt dizzy. "Would you like to read?" he asked hesitantly. I opened the book to page 125. My mouth was dry. My eyes began to water. I could not begin. "You can read later," Mr. Lema said understandingly.

For the rest of the reading period I kept getting angrier and angrier with myself. I should have read, I thought to myself.

During recess I went into the rest room and opened my English book to page 125. I began to read in a low voice, pretending I was in class. There were many words I did not know. I closed the book and headed back to the classroom.

Mr. Lema was sitting at his desk correcting papers. When I entered he looked up at me and smiled. I felt better. I walked up to him and asked if he could help me with the new words. "Gladly," he said.

The rest of the month I spent my lunch hours working on English with Mr. Lema, my best friend at school.

One Friday during lunch hour Mr. Lema asked me to take a walk with him to the music room. "Do you like music?" he asked me as we entered the building.

8. A turning point is the place in a story where the plot moves in a new direction. Why could this be a turning point for Panchito?

"Yes, I like *corridos*,"* I answered. He then picked up a trumpet, blew on it, and handed it to me. The sound gave me goose bumps. I knew that sound. I had heard it in many corridos. "How would you like to learn how to play it?" he asked. He must have read my face because before I could answer, he added, "I'll teach you how to play it during our lunch hours."

That day I could hardly wait to get home to tell Papá and Mamá the great news. As I got off the bus, my little brothers and sisters ran up to meet me. They were yelling and screaming. I thought they were happy to see me, but when I opened the door to our shack, I saw that everything we owned was neatly packed in cardboard boxes.

9. Recall what the neatly packed cardboard boxes symbolize to Panchito. Will Panchito go to school tomorrow? Why or why not?

* *corridos*: a type of Mexican folk music.

Present the Story

Charting Motivation ■ ■ ■

Discuss with students that the reasons why a character acts a certain way or does a certain thing can often be attributed to the character's *motivation*. Motivation often includes a goal. Recall the characters from the three previous stories in this book and analyze their motivations, as shown in the chart below. You might start a similar chart on poster paper to serve as a visual cue to prompt students' ideas.

Then share with students that in the story they are about to read, they will meet a boy named Panchito and his family. As they read, ask students to look for the things that motivate Panchito as well as the things that motivate his family. Have them complete the chart with their ideas.

Analyzing Motivation

Story Character	Goal	Actions
Manuel	to make his family proud; to impress a girl	volunteers to be in a talent show
Pierre	to work with his horse, Joseph	hides his blindness as he works
Pearl	to cope with her mother's death; to not be a burden to others	does not speak
Mary	to help other children in need; to cope with the death of her children	forms the Frontier Nursing Service
Panchito	to go to school	bonds with Mr. Lema
Panchito's family	to support the family	moves from farm to farm for work

Distribute Copies of the Story ■ ■ ■

Pass out the story, and invite students to briefly flip through the pages. Share with students that this story is similar to "How Many Stars in My Crown?" because it is also told from the first-person point of view. In this story, we view the action from Panchito's point of view, a Mexican boy living in California. As students glance through the pages, point out the words followed by asterisks and the corresponding footnotes. Explain that some words in the story are Spanish, and the footnotes provide translations.

⸪ Read the Story

As students read the story together, refer to the margin notes to guide discussion.

Margin Note 1:

What is the story <u>setting</u>? What do you think a *sharecropper* is?

Student Response: The story appears to take place on a farm. A sharecropper appears to be someone who works on the farm.

Further Discussion: Confirm students' ideas. Further explain that the story takes place on farms in California. Workers often flock to the farms during harvest times, where they are paid to help the farmer pick the ripe fruits and vegetables. A sharecropper usually doesn't own the farmland on which he works. Instead, he gives a portion, or a "share," of the crop to the landowner.

Margin Note 2:

The <u>mood</u> is the feelings you get from the descriptive words and the characters' actions. What is the <u>mood</u> at this point in the story?

Student Response: The mood seems tired and sad.

Further Discussion: Encourage students to read phrases that set up this mood, or atmosphere, such as "the sun had tired and sunk behind the mountains," "Those were the words I waited for twelve hours a day, every day, seven days a week, week after week," "the thought . . . saddened me."

Margin Note 3:

The "neatly packed cardboard boxes" <u>symbolize</u> something to Panchito. What might it be?

Student Response: The boxes symbolize that it is time to move again.

Further Discussion: Talk with students about how Panchito feels about moving. Is he excited and anxious? Does he view it as an adventure? Help students conclude that Panchito instead feels tired and weary. In fact, he even explains how much he hates the move.

Margin Note 4:

This paragraph <u>characterizes</u> Papá. After reading this paragraph, how would you describe Papá?

Student Response: Papá seems very responsible and careful about the money he spends. He is a proud man, but modest.

Further Discussion: Point out to students that the author has devoted a very long paragraph to the car's description and purchase. What other information do we learn in this paragraph? Point out the dates—the car was made in 1938, and the car was bought in 1949. What does this tell us about the setting of the story? (The story was set about 50 years ago.) What conclusions can they draw about someone who buys an 11-year-old car? (They probably don't have enough money to afford a new car.)

Margin Note 5:

What do you think the *olla* <u>symbolizes</u> to Mamá?

Student Response: The pot probably symbolizes the joys and hardships of the family.

Further Discussion: Encourage students to share their ideas, then suggest that perhaps each dent and nick in the pot symbolizes challenges the family has overcome. The pot is still there, and so is the family, strong and able.

Margin Note 6:

What words could you use to describe the <u>setting</u> of this paragraph?

Student Response: Accept all reasonable responses, such as *very hot, scorching, suffocating, humid, unbearable,* and so on.

Further Discussion: Let students react to Panchito's plight in the vineyard. How would they feel if they were in Panchito's place? Why do they think his family makes him work in the vineyard when it is so hot? What does this tell us about the situation of Panchito's family?

Margin Note 7:

Panchito has mixed feelings about going to school. This is an <u>inner conflict.</u> Why is he happy to go to school? Why does he hide his happiness?

Student Response: Panchito is happy to go to school because he doesn't have to work, and he wants to start sixth grade. However, he does not want to show his happiness in front of his brother, who can not go to school.

Further Discussion: Speculate with students how Panchito's conflict here might come back later in the story. Why might Panchito's longing to go to school be in conflict with something his family must do?

Margin Note 8:

A <u>turning point</u> is the place in a story where the plot moves in a new direction. Why could this be a <u>turning point</u> for Panchito?

Student Response: It could be a turning point for Panchito because he feels like he is succeeding and that he finally belongs.

Further Discussion: Suggest that Panchito's first day of school was also a turning point. The plot turned in another direction as Panchito's days of working in the vineyard ended and his days of school began.

Margin Note 9:

Recall what the neatly packed cardboard boxes <u>symbolize</u> to Panchito. Will Panchito go to school tomorrow? Why or why not?

Student Response: The packed boxes symbolize that the family must once again move. Panchito will not be going back to school because the family must move.

Further Discussion: Again, lead students to realize that the author doesn't tell us that Panchito must move. We gather this information by recalling the symbolism of the packed boxes. Also conclude with students that the packed boxes are not happy symbols for Panchito. Speculate how Panchito must feel.

Analyze the Story— As a Group

Affective Response ■ ■ ■

Reproduce and pass out copies of page 80, Personal Responses. Review the questions with the class and let students freely discuss their ideas and impressions. As an alternate activity, encourage students to discuss the story in small groups, using the questions on the sheet to guide their discussions. Monitor the group discussions and intercede as necessary.

Refer to the motivation chart you shared with students before reading. Discuss with students the goals and resulting actions of Panchito and his family. Point out that the characters' motivations are like the "engine" that drives the story along. Characters behave and take action according to their goals, or things that "drive" or motivate them.

Literal Response ■ ■ ■

Initiate a discussion about story setting, inviting students to compare the setting of this story with the setting of "La Bamba." Draw a Venn diagram on the chalkboard, like the one shown on the next page. Challenge students to complete the diagram by deciding what the story settings have in common, then how the story settings differ. Suggest to students that the story setting is almost like an additional "character." The main characters act and relate within the setting, sometimes acting and relating *to* the setting as well.

Setting

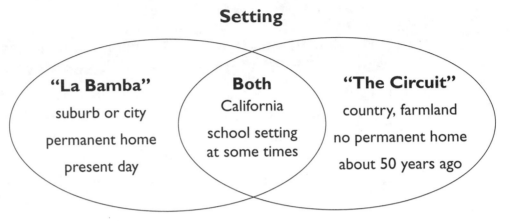

"La Bamba"
suburb or city
permanent home
present day

Both
California
school setting
at some times

"The Circuit"
country, farmland
no permanent home
about 50 years ago

EXPLORING LITERARY ELEMENTS

Write the word *circuit* on the chalkboard and challenge students to define it. You might let a volunteer look up the word in a dictionary, confirming that one definition is "a regular route around an assigned area or district." Discuss with students why this word is an appropriate title for the story, concluding that the family makes a "circuit" each year as they follow the seasonal harvest cycle of the crops, looking for work.

Then ask a student to read aloud the third sentence in the fifth paragraph of the story: "Everything we owned was neatly packed in cardboard boxes." Ask another student to read the last sentence of the story. Point out that the two sentences are exactly the same. Speculate why the author might have chosen to write these words in the same way. Explain that the repetition emphasizes that Panchito is caught up in a "circuit" which he can't seem to break, no matter what may be going on in his life outside the family.

To further emphasize the significance and symbolism of the circuit, encourage students to diagram the story as a plot wheel. Ahead of time, prepare the plot wheel on page 77 on chart paper. Encourage students to help you fill in each "spoke" of the wheel. Have students notice that the plot wheel shows how the story comes "full circle," leading Panchito—and the readers—back to the beginning of the story.

Possible answers have been provided in this plot wheel. However, except for the headings, leave the plot wheel blank, challenging students to arrive at the answers themselves. Point out to students that the plot wheel follows the story sequence of events. Reproduce and pass out the plot wheel activity on page 81. Encourage students to complete the plot wheel for "The Circuit."

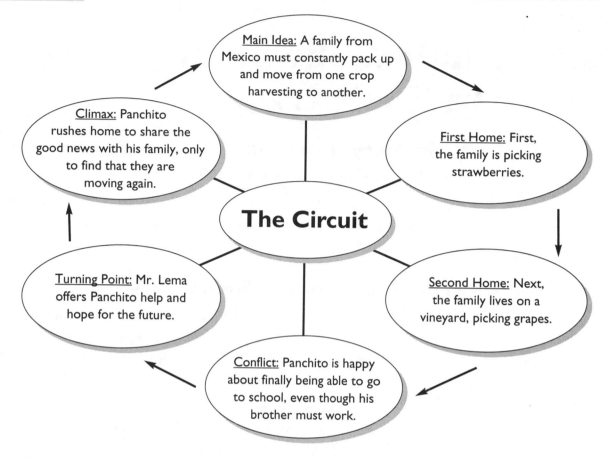

Challenge: Comparing Themes ■ ■ ■

Invite a student to read the definition for *theme* found in the glossary of this book. Explain that a theme is almost like a secret message the author is trying to tell the reader, using the story characters as examples. On the chalkboard, start a chart like the one shown here. Challenge students to compose a sentence for each story that reflects its theme.

Comparing Themes

Story Title	Author	Main Character	Theme
"La Bamba"	Gary Soto	Manuel	The twists and turns of fate may bring you unexpected rewards.
"A Secret for Two"	Quentin Reynolds	Pierre	There can be more to a situation than first meets the eye.
"How Many Stars in My Crown?"	Rosemary Wells	Pearl	We can learn from life's tragedies and become stronger because of them.
"The Circuit"	Francisco Jimenez	Panchito	We can't always control our destinies, but we must learn to deal with them.

Analyze the Story— On Their Own

Retell the Story—Plot Points ▪▪▪

To focus on plot, invite students to:

◆ Retell the story as they explain its title, "The Circuit." Make sure students understand why "The Circuit" is an appropriate title and how it relates to Panchito and his work and school situation.

Retell the Story—Another Format ▪▪▪

◆ To focus on setting and atmosphere, encourage students to write poems that describe a scene from the story. Challenge students to write their poems from the first-person point of view, or from Panchito's point of view. Stress to students that their poems can rhyme, but they don't have to. For example:

> Smothered in a blanket of heat,
> I watched the cool kids flow out of the school bus.
> Hiding in the shadows of the vines,
> I wished I could join them in the sunlight.

◆ To focus on character, suggest that students pretend to be Panchito and Mr. Lema, exchanging letters. Have students work with partners, asking each to take a role. Then instruct students to write and exchange an initial letter that explains how much the letter-writer appreciated that story character. If time allows, let students respond to each other's letters.

◆ To focus on plot, ask the class to brainstorm some events that might take place if Panchito ever returns to Mr. Lema's school—for example, to start seventh grade. To guide their writing and plot points, make copies of the plot wheel from page 81 for students to fill in with their plot ideas.

Plan an Original Story ▪▪▪

Plot Reproduce and pass out the planning sheet from page 82, Developing a Story Plot. Review that a plot needs to have:

1. The main idea. This should be the first thing students come up with when plotting a story. Student writers should consider that the main idea is like the foundation of the story upon which the plot is built and developed.

2. The complications. These are any problems that must be solved, or any conflicts characters must resolve.

3. The climax. This is the point in the story that all events have been leading up to. The climax could be when the problem or conflict reaches a peak, right before the solution is apparent.

4. The resolution. This is how the problem is solved, how the conflict is resolved. It is the end of the story.

Theme Remind students that each of the stories they read in this book has a theme, or a universal message or lesson they could learn upon reading the story. Suggest that students choose a theme from one of these four stories and write a new story around it. For example, suppose their theme for "The Circuit" was "Sometimes your responsibilities take you away from your bigger goals." How might this theme be appropriate for, say, a fairy-tale princess or prince? an astronaut, who wants to blast off into space? or something closer to home, such as a family member who has sacrificed a personal goal for the sake of the family?

Story Action Photographs, paintings, and newspaper or magazine pictures are ideal for prompting students' creative-writing ideas. In a large, oversize art book, find classic paintings that suggest movement and emotion, such as Breughel's "Children at Play," Winslow Homer's "The Gulf Stream," or Giorgio De Chirico's "The Melancholy and Mystery of a Street." Photographs from newspapers and magazines that show ordinary, unidentified people interacting and moving are also useful and may be more easily accessible. You might briefly discuss with the class what is happening in each picture. Then encourage students to work independently to draft a story that the picture suggests to them.

Share your Writing ■ ■ ■

Let students review, assess, and revise their stories following the Writing Partner procedure. (See the reproducible on page 87). Or try the following:

How and Why. In this sharing strategy, the student writer reads the story draft aloud to a small group. Classmates then discuss, amongst themselves while the writer listens, issues that puzzle them. For example:

> I don't understand why Eva suddenly cares about George's problem. How does Eva find out that George likes horses? How does George's horse escape from the barn? Why does the horse finally come home?

A challenge is presented to both the writer and the listeners. The listeners must mold their comments in noncritical ways, expressing only their confusion or uncertainty about the plot. The writer must remain silent while classmates discuss and question the story, jotting down notes. Upon revising the story, the writer could read the story to the same group of classmates, asking them if the revision has solved the confusing issues.

Story 4   The Circuit

Personal Responses

1. After reading a story, readers often come away with deep feelings for it, or an "emotional response." Describe your emotional response to this story.

_____

_____

_____

_____

2. Imagine you are Panchito. How do you feel about your family's life? Why do you feel this way?

_____

_____

_____

_____

_____

3. The word *school* holds a different meaning for different children. What does *school* stand for from Panchito's point of view?

_____

_____

_____

_____

4. Imagine you are a friend of Panchito's from his new school. What would you say to Panchito when he has to move again?

_____

_____

_____

_____

Name .... Date ....

∴ Plot Wheel ∵

Think about the story "The Circuit." Fill in the plot wheel below to show how the story develops.

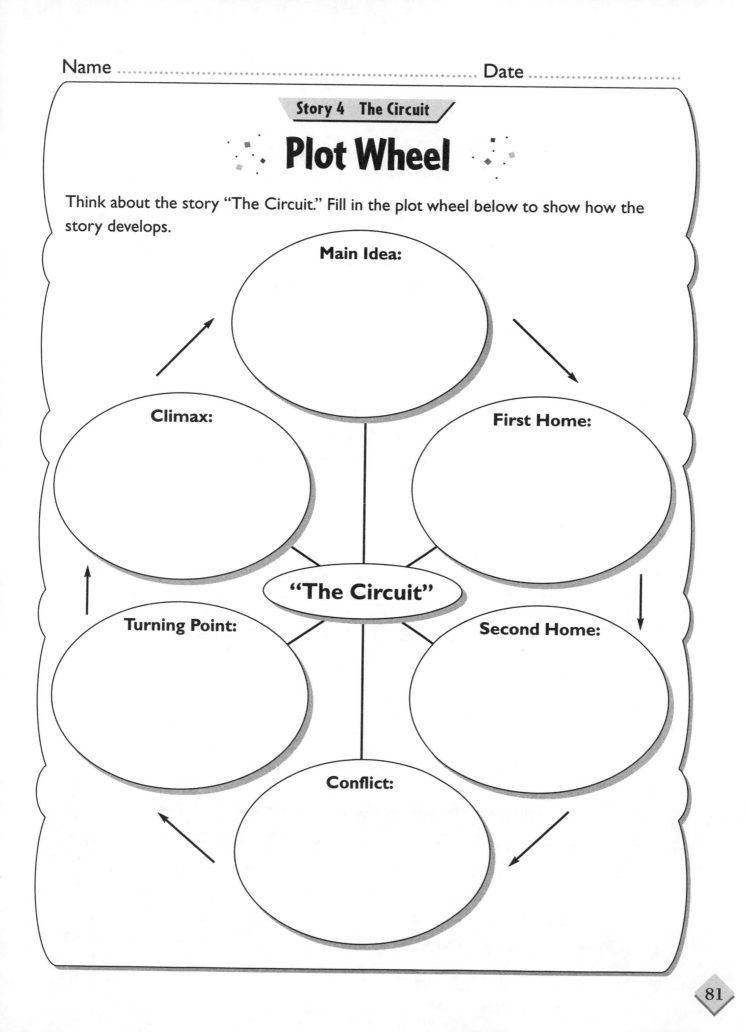

Main Idea:

Climax:

First Home:

"The Circuit"

Turning Point:

Second Home:

Conflict:

Name .... Date ....

Developing a Story Plot

Use the chart below to help you create a plot for a story of your own.

Main Idea

What will this story be about? Include the characters and setting.

_____

_____

_____

_____

Complications

What problem or conflict does the story character face?

_____

_____

_____

_____

Climax

How does the action of the story build to a peak?

_____

_____

_____

_____

Resolution

How does the character solve/resolve the problem/conflict?

_____

_____

_____

_____

Name .... Date ....

Story Summaries

In this section are my copies of the following stories:

La Bamba by Gary Soto
Story Summary:

_____

_____

_____

_____

_____

A Secret for Two by Quentin Reynolds
Story Summary:

_____

_____

_____

_____

_____

_____

How Many Stars in My Crown? by Rosemary Wells
Story Summary:

_____

_____

_____

_____

_____

The Circuit by Francisco Jimenez
Story Summary:

_____

_____

_____

_____

_____

Name .... Date ....

Personal Responses

In this section are my personal responses for each story.

La Bamba by Gary Soto
How This Story Made Me Feel:

_____
_____
_____
_____
_____

A Secret for Two by Quentin Reynolds
How This Story Made Me Feel:

_____
_____
_____
_____
_____

How Many Stars in My Crown? by Rosemary Wells
How This Story Made Me Feel:

_____
_____
_____
_____
_____

The Circuit by Francisco Jimenez
How This Story Made Me Feel:

_____
_____
_____
_____
_____

Name .... Date ....

Story Planning

In this section are my Story Planning activity sheets. This chart explains what I found to be easy and challenging about each.

Activity Sheet	What Was Easy About This	What Was Challenging About This
Developing a Main Character		
Developing a Story Setting		
Practicing Characterizations		
Developing a Story Plot		

Name .... Date ....

Story Drafts

In this section are the first drafts for some of my stories.

Story Title	A One-Sentence Story Summary	Story Elements I Think Need Work
1.		
2.		
3.		
4.		

Name .... Date ....

Writing Partner Conference

The title of my story: _____

My writing partner's ideas:

1. The character(s). _____

_____

_____

_____

2. The setting. _____

_____

_____

_____

3. The plot. _____

_____

_____

_____

4. Other comments and suggestions: _____

_____

_____

_____

5. How this conference helped my story: _____

_____

_____

_____

_____

Name .... Date ....

Completed Stories

In this section are my revised and completed stories.

Story Title	Revisions I Made	How the Revisions Made the Story Better
1.		
2.		
3.		
4.		

Name .... Date ....

Comments About Other Short Stories

Complete the chart below to tell about other short stories you have read. Explain which story element, such as the main character, setting, or plot, you enjoyed the most. Write your own description of that story element.

Story Title and Author	Story Element I Enjoyed the Most	My Description of the Story Element
1.		
2.		
3.		
4.		

Glossary of Literary Elements

ATMOSPHERE

Atmosphere is the general feeling or mood in a work of literature. Writers create atmosphere by using imagery and descriptions. Readers can describe atmosphere in just a word or two—for example, "a *scary* poem," "an *exciting* scene," "a story filled with *sadness*."

CHARACTER

A character is a person or an animal in a work of literature. A character can even be a thing—for example, the stuffed toy in *The Velveteen Rabbit* or the computer in the movie *2001: A Space Odyssey*.

CHARACTERIZATION

Characterization is *how* the writer reveals what a character is like. Writers do this in different ways:

Direct Characterization: The writer simply tells what the character is like. Example: Jamie had a hot temper and a tender heart.

Indirect Characterization: The writer gives the actual words of the character, tells what the character is thinking and feeling, tells about the character's actions, or tells how others respond to the character. Example:

> Jamie threw his lunch box across the room, then burst into tears.
> "I'm sorry!" he wailed. "I'm just so tired of peanut butter!"

CLIMAX

Climax is the exciting point in the story where the main character or characters face and make a huge decision. For readers, the climax is usually the most suspenseful part of the story. It's the point where the conflict will finally be settled. The climax occurs toward the end of the story.

COMPLICATIONS

The complications are the things the character must deal with as she or he tries to solve the conflict.

CONFLICT

The conflict is the major struggle between characters or between opposing forces. A conflict may be *external* or *internal*. Some stories have both kinds of conflict.

<u>External Conflict</u>: The main character struggles with another person or with an outside force, like the sea.

<u>Internal Conflict</u>: The main character struggles with opposing ideas or feelings within his or her own mind, like wanting to make friends at a new school but also being very shy.

DIALOGUE

Dialogue consists of the exact words that characters say. When you write dialogue, you use quotation marks to enclose the exact words. Example:

"Don't even try to climb the mountain!" said Luis.

"Why not?" replied Shana. "I like challenges!"

IMAGERY

Imagery is language that appeals to the senses. Examples:

a freezing-cold snow cone; the fragile and gentle touch of a butterfly's wings; the screeching cry of an owl

INTRODUCTION

The introduction is the beginning of the story. It starts the plot moving by grabbing the reader's attention. An introduction can name the main character, describe the setting, and perhaps even the conflict. Example:

A long time ago, a girl named Cinderella sat by the fireside. She was a sweet girl and hard worker, but her sisters and stepmother treated her badly.

METAPHOR

A metaphor is a word or phrase that draws a comparison between two things. It does not use the words *like* or *as;* therefore, it is often harder to identify than a simile. Metaphors may not be factually true, but they help readers see events and characters in a vivid way. Example:

His eyes are *piercing lasers.*

MOTIVATION

Motivation is *why* characters behave in a certain way. As a reader, you can track motivation with *because* sentences. Examples:

Manuel entered the talent show because he wanted to impress a girl he liked.

Shana befriended the new student because Shana remembered how awful it felt to be an outsider.

PLOT

Plot is the series of related events that make up the story. Most plots go this way:

The *introduction* tells who the main characters are and what the main conflict is.

Complications develop as characters do things to try to solve the conflict.

In the *climax,* the main characters make a final decision that solves the conflict.

The story ends with a *resolution:* the writer tells what the main characters feel or do now that the conflict is settled.

POINT OF VIEW

Point of view in a literary work is the vantage point from which the story is told. Two common points of view are the first-person point of view and the all-knowing, or omniscient, point of view. Examples:

<u>First-person Point of View</u>: The person telling the story is often a character in the story. The character uses such words as *I, me, mine, myself.* The first-person narrator only tells what she or he observes or experiences.

"I sympathized with Leah and asked her to sit with me at my table."

<u>All-knowing Point of View</u>: The person telling the story is *not* a character. This "third person" uses third-person pronouns, such as *she, he, her, him, they.*

"He sympathized with Leah and asked her to sit at his table."

RESOLUTION

The resolution occurs at the end of the story. Often, it includes how the main character feels about experiences faced in the story.

SETTING

The setting is the time, place, and atmosphere in which a story's events occur.

SIMILE

A simile is a description that compares one thing to another, using the words *like* or *as.* Similes may not be factually true, but they help readers to see events and characters in a vivid way. Example:

The hurricane was *like a huge beast trying to devour us.*

SETTING

Something (an object or color, for example) that an author uses to represent an idea in a story.

THEME

The theme is the big idea that a story conveys about life. The writer usually doesn't state the theme directly. It's up to the readers to discover the theme for themselves. Some stories may also have more than one theme.

Bibliography

This bibliography provides just a few titles from the many collections of short stories available to you and your students. We hope that the variety of titles and the book descriptions will encourage you to cast your net wide as you look for examples to enjoy with your class. Whether they're brief tales set in modern schools, science-fiction adventures, retellings of Arthurian legends, trickster tales from Africa, or stand-alone episodes in chapter books, good short stories will reveal to your students again and again the elements that make literature memorable.

Avi. *What Do Fish Have to Do with Anything? And Other Stories.* (Candlewick, 1997). These seven stories zero in on adolescents who move beyond self-absorption and discover that they can plan and follow a course of action.

Barrett, Peter A., ed. *To Break the Silence: Thirteen Short Stories for Young Readers.* (Dell, 1986). This book includes stories from some of the most popular children's writers, including Joan Aiken, E.L. Konigsburg, Katherine Paterson, Jill Paton Walsh, Langston Hughes, and others. All the stories are wonderful, especially "Thank You, Ma'am" by Langston Hughes, and the surreal mystery "A Room Full of Leaves" by Joan Aiken.

Blos, Joan W. *Brooklyn Doesn't Rhyme.* (Scribners, 1994). Set in the early 1900s, these stories are vignettes from the journal of Rosy, a sixth grader, who tells about her extended family and herself.

Bruchac, Joseph. *Native American Stories.* (Fulcrum, 1991). Twenty-four tales of Native American origin, retold by Bruchac. Many of the stories are *pourquoi* tales, or "why" stories, that explain a natural phenomenon. Many young writers like to give this type of story a try.

Burandt, Harriet, and **Shelley Dale.** *Tales from the Homeplace: Adventures of a Texas Farm Girl.* (Holt, 1997). Nine sketches of life in a Texas farm family during the Depresssion. The stories are told from the point of view of Irene, the oldest girl. The stories are based on true incidents.

Cofer, Judith Ortiz. *An Island Like You: Stories of the Barrio.* (Orchard, 1995). These stories have a continuity of setting: a Puerto Rican neighborhood in New Jersey. Also, characters from one story are apt to appear in another as well.

Conrad, Pam. *Our House: The Stories of Levittown.* (Scholastic, 1995). Levittown was post–World War II's model "housing development." The six short stories, and the great drawings, show the "development" growing into a true community over the years.

Coville, Bruce. *Odder Than Ever.* (Harcourt, 1999). This anthology contains six previously published stories and three new ones from the popular sci-fi writer. The tales range from scary to tounge-in-cheek funny.

Ellis, Sarah. *Back of Beyond.* (McElderry, 1998). Eerie stories, sure to intrigue and entertain your class.

Gantos, Jack. *Jack's New Power: Stories from a Caribbean Year.* (Farrar, 1996). Told from the first-person point of view of a 12-year-old-boy, these stories center around the boy and his family living in Barbados. Also try *Jack's Black Box* (1997), in which Jack, now at the end of seventh grade, decides on a writing career.

Glass, Tim. *Even a Little Is Something: Stories of Nong.* (Linnet, 1998). Nong is an 11-year-old girl in Thailand. These stories show her rich interactions with the people of her village.

Issacs, Anne. *Treehouse Tales.* (Dutton, 1997). Three amusing tales, set in Pennsylvania in the 1880s, follow three farm children—Tom, Emily, and Natty—as they grow up.

Lester, Julius. *How Many Spots Does a Leopard Have?* (Scholastic, 1989). Twelve tales from Jewish and African cultures. Of great additional value, this book contains extensive notes and a bibliography.

McCaughrean, Geraldine. *A Pack of Lies.* (Scholastic, 1988). A collection of linked short stories that all together have the feel of a novel.

Peck, Richard. *A Long Way from Chicago: A Novel in Stories.* (Dial, 1998). Grandma Dowdel, an unconventional grandmother, tells entertaining stories to her awed grandchildren. The time is the Depression, the place is a small town, and this whole setting is marvelously captured.

Perham, Molly. *King Arthur and the Legends of Camelot.* (Viking, 1993). Most of the major figures and myths from the King Arthur tales, such as Merlin, Lancelot, Guinevere, and the quest for the Holy Grail, can be found in this story collection.

Philip, Neil. *American Fairy Tales: From Rip Van Winkle to the Rootabaga Stories.* (Hyperion, 1997). A dozen short stories in the fairy-tale tradition. A good resource for its selective bibliography.

Porte, Barbara Ann. *Hearsay: Strange Tales from the Middle Kingdom.* (Greenwillow, 1998). In this collection, you will find 15 stories, drawn from the folklore of China. Some are legends, and some are the author's own.

Ross, Gayle. *How Rabbit Tricked Otter.* (HarperCollins, 1994). These 15 Cherokee tales feature Rabbit as the trickster and include variants found in African-American traditional stories.

Rosselson, Leon. *Rosa and Her Singing Grandfather.* (Philomel, 1996). In each chapter of this episodic book, readers learn about the problems and pleasures of Rosa, whose grandfather bursts into song in a variety of situations.

Spells of Enchantment: The Wondrous Fairy Tales of Western Culture. (Viking, 1992). A comprehensive collection, featuring more than 60 stories. Tales range from the 2nd century to modern times.

Spinelli, Jerry. *The Library Card.* (Scholastic, 1997). Four stories that center on the protagonist's adventures with a library card. Some tales are humorous, others are melancholy.

Trevor, William. *Juliet's Story.* (Simon, 1994). Students will enjoy traveling through Europe with Juliet and her grandmother, who tells her marvelous tales that help Juliet find her own story.

Vande Velde, Vivian. *Tales from the Brothers Grimm and the Sisters Weird.* (Harcourt, 1996). Amusing—and sometimes touching—versions of old favorites. For example, in "The Granddaughter," Red Riding Hood manages to drive both the Wolf and her grandmother completely up the wall.

Watkins, Yoko Kawashima. *Tales from the Bamboo Grove.* (Bradbury, 1992). These six stories are the same tales told around the dinner table by the author's family when she was a young girl.

Wynne-Jones, Tim. *The Book of Changes.* (Orchard, 1995); *Some of the Kinder Planets.* (Orchard, 1995, winner of the Boston Globe-Horn Book Award); and *Lord of the Fries.* (Krouper/DK Ink, 1999). Margaret Willey considers Wynne-Jones "the master of the glimpse." His stories reveal human nature with fun and originality.

Yolen, Jane, ed. *Camelot: A Collection of Original Arthurian Tales.* (Putnam, 1995). Students will enjoy these original stories based on characters from the King Arthur legend by such notable writers as Terry Pratchett, James MacDonald, and Anne McCaffrey.